INTERVIEWING

ITS PRINCIPLES AND METHODS

By

Annette Garrett

Associate Director, Smith College
School for Social Work

FAMILY SOCIAL WORK
FAMILY LIFE

FAMILY WELFARE ASSOCIATION OF AMERICA
122 East 22d Street, New York, N. Y.

Printed Through the Henry H. Bonnell Fund

FOREWORD

SKILL in interviewing is prerequisite in many types of research and business and professional service. As the author remarks, practically all of us interview or get interviewed, and many people are eager to increase their skill in this medium through which so much information is secured and given and so many plans are made.

Interviews are the primary medium through which social services are given. In the field of social work called social case work, which gives individualized service to people, methods of interviewing (or discussing plans or counseling with people) have long been a subject of study. Detailed records of interviews are kept by social case work agencies as a record of the agency's work and a means for the study and development of professional skills.

The Publications Department of the Family Welfare Association of America, which publishes social work literature, receives more requests for material on "how to interview" and for examples of good interviews than on any other subject. These requests come not only from social workers but also from schools and colleges, research workers, counselors, members of other professions and volunteer groups. In response to this demand, this book was planned for the use both of case workers and of interviewers in other kinds of organizations. While the discussion and most of the examples included are based on social case work experience, the study is not offered as a text on the techniques of case work but is focused on interviewing methods as such.

In Part One the author formulates for us the principles and methods of interviewing used in social case work. This section discusses, in a clear and helpful way, many practical questions, such as how to begin and end an interview, when to ask questions, to listen, or to comment, when to take notes. As a background the author discusses briefly but pertinently the psychology of human nature in terms of the feelings and attitudes people have about their difficulties and their reactions in the interviewing process. Warmth of interest in people and a sincere desire to be helpful, respect for the other person's feelings and his capacity to make his own plans, perceptive observation and sensitive understanding, and skill in counseling — all are essential for good interviewing and can be developed by thoughtful study and experience.

Part Two contains illustrative interviews, annotated with comments applying the principles and methods discussed in Part One. A number of social case work agencies were asked to contribute to this project by sending samples of current interviews illustrating various problems confronting people in these days and the methods of interviewing. From these, the author selected seven of the nine interviews reproduced. We wish to express our appreciation to the following contributing agencies: Family Welfare Society, Boston, Mass., Psychiatric Social Work Unit of the Massachusetts State Selective Service Headquarters, Boston, Mass., Boston Urban League, Boston, Mass., Family Welfare Association of Springfield, Mass., Family Welfare Association, Minneapolis, Minn., Family Service Society of St. Louis County, Clayton, Missouri, Family Service Association, Trenton, N. J., Department of Social Service of the Long Island College Hospital, Brooklyn, N. Y., Young Women's Christian Association, Brooklyn, N. Y., Department of Public Welfare, City of New Rochelle, N. Y., Community Service Society, Bureau for Men and Boys, New York, N. Y., Free Synagogue Child Adoption Committee, New York, N. Y., National Travelers Aid Association, New York, N. Y., New York Association for Jewish Children, New York, N. Y., Travelers Aid Society, New York, N. Y., American Service Institute of Allegheny County, Pittsburgh, Pa. We also wish to express our appreciation for the permissions to reprint material in Chapters VI, VIII, and XVI, granted by Harvard University Press, Cambridge, Mass., the *Atlantic Monthly*, Boston, and Little, Brown and Company, Boston.

MAURINE LA BARRE
Editor, F. W.A.A. Publications

CONTENTS

PART ONE: THE NATURE OF INTERVIEWING

PART TWO: SELECTED INTERVIEWS

RECAPITULATION

PART ONE

THE NATURE OF INTERVIEWING

I.

THE ART OF INTERVIEWING

EVERYONE engages in interviewing. Sometimes he interviews; sometimes he is interviewed. The mother interviews the principal of the school in which she is thinking of entering her son. He, in turn, interviews the mother and the boy. Later the boy is interviewed by his prospective employer and, in turn, interviews the latter. Some people, because of the nature of their work, spend a good deal of time in interviewing. The attendant in an information booth devotes all his working hours to miniature interviews. Lawyers, doctors, nurses, newspapermen, policemen, ministers, counselors, credit men, personnel managers, employers, all devote a considerable amount of time to talking with people, getting information from them, advising them, helping them. They acquire various degrees of skill in the art of interviewing, sometimes consciously, usually unconsciously. One group who are interviewers *par excellence* are social case workers. Their tasks make them professional interviewers, and for some of them interviewing becomes an art, and, indeed, almost a science, some of whose basic principles at least they are able to formulate and organize into the beginnings of a systematic body of knowledge.

Probably everyone starting to interview wishes there were a list of rules he could follow, but, unfortunately, it is impossible to enumerate a complete list of infallible rules for all interviewing, or even for any particular kind. Interviewing takes place between human beings who are much too individualized to be reduced to a formula. To be sure, there are certain psychological traits which characterize most people most of the time, and a skilled interviewer will do well to keep some of the more important of these in mind. There are characteristic modes of human action and reaction, and awareness of them tends to increase the satisfactoriness of one's relationships with others. Interviewing in-

7

volves a closer and subtler relation between human beings than may at first be recognized, and skill in conducting this relationship can be increased through knowledge of the fundamental factors involved.

Some people fear that a self-conscious study of the principles of interviewing may detract from the warm friendliness and real interest in other individuals which are so essential for the successful practice of the art. There is certainly no necessity for this to be the case. An informed person need not be unfriendly. One need not be ignorant of human psychology to love human beings. Indeed the opposite is often true. There are few things so frustrating as to love someone but not know how to give the help he desperately needs; and contrariwise, to be able to help those we love increases our affection for them.

Warm human interest does sometimes vanish from interviewing, and when that happens it becomes a monotonous, mechanical sort of thing that is relatively valueless. But the cause of this, when it occurs, is not knowledge of the rich interplay of one human mind with another but the ignorance that regards interviewing as a routine affair of asking set questions and recording answers. If this were all there were to interviewing, a phonograph with a recording device would serve the purpose far better. But with a proper understanding of even some of the intricacies of human personality and of the effective give and take between two complex human beings, our attention and warm interest are aroused in increasing measure, and the process becomes anything but routine.

Interviewing is an art, a skilled technique which can be improved and eventually perfected primarily through continued practice. But mere practice alone is not enough. Skills can be developed to their fullest potentialities only when practice is accompanied by knowledge about interviewing and self-conscious study of our own practice. Knowledge of the theory underlying interviewing gives us certain material in the light of which we can critically examine our present techniques and discern ways in which they can be improved.

The obvious fact about interviewing is that it involves communication between two people. It might be called professional conversation. Special problems confront both interviewer and interviewee. We begin to obtain some notion of the complexities involved if we recall some of the feelings we ourselves have had while on the way to be interviewed. Perhaps we were seeking to borrow money, were consulting a doctor or a lawyer, or were applying for a job. We may have felt some fear at the prospect of talking with an unknown person and of revealing our

needs to him. We may have been uncertain as to just what about ourselves we might have to tell, fearful that he might wish to know more
than we were willing to relate, might not understand us, or might not
grant our request.

On the other hand, when we first began to interview, what were
some of the worries that plagued us? Would we say the right things to
put our client at his ease? Would we be able to draw him out? What
would we do if he didn't talk, and if he did, would we be sure to select
the significant facts in his remarks and behavior?

For an interview to be successful, the diverse fears of both interviewer and interviewee must be allayed, and the diverse desires of both
must be met. Rapport must be established between the two, a relationship that will enable the interviewee to reveal the essential facts of his
situation and that will enable the interviewer to be most effective in
helping him.

Preview

To give meaning and background to the suggestions for interviewing which we make later, and to enable the interviewer to carry out
these suggestions with understanding, we shall devote our next chapter
to a study of certain basic facts about human nature, concentrating our
attention on those that are most significant for interviewing. The following comments indicate the special areas that will be discussed in
some detail.

Although most of us feel the need at times of going to a lawyer or
physician for expert knowledge, we tend to feel that we already possess an adequate working knowledge of the nature of human beings
and their behavior. But such knowledge is likely to be a combination of
old wives' maxims and generalizations based on our own necessarily
limited experience and distorted by our own peculiar blind spots. We
interpret others in terms of ourselves, forgetting that our own view is
influenced by a host of more or less concealed prejudices and emotions.

Interviewers should have more than casual knowledge of the important role in human motivation of influences other than the conscious
and the rational. They should apply this knowledge to an understanding not only of their clients' personalities, needs, prejudices, and emotions, but also of their own. The wise maxim of the ancient Greeks,
"Know thyself," applies especially to interviewers.

The fact that an interviewer's attention must continuously be directed in two ways, toward himself as well as toward his client, some-

times makes him fear that he may become so overly self-conscious in his responses and may lose so much of his natural human warmth that his client will be alienated. But he soon learns to see the contrary danger, that spontaneous and unselfconscious response may be recognized by the client as only a surface response supported by such insufficient understanding of his real feelings that effective help will be impossible.

Another chapter is devoted to a discussion of the purposes of interviews. They take place for all sorts of reasons. At one end of the scale is the interview of the census-taker whose one immediate purpose is simply to obtain specific information. At the opposite end is the definitely therapeutic interviewing of the psychiatrist or psychoanalyst. Between lies the vast majority of interviews where the aim is to help in one way or another, and information is sought primarily to point this help at actual needs and to make it effective.

It is impossible to discuss interviewing in a vacuum. The specific techniques of interviewing vary, of course, with the purpose in mind. Since nearly all interviews involve the obtaining of information for the purpose of helping people, we use, as typical examples, interviews of this kind on a professional level, interviews characteristic of general social case work. Such interviewing furnishes rich material for a discussion of the nature and methods of the art. Another advantage of choosing this general field is that applications to specific fields of interviewing can readily be made.

Since we approach interviewing from its setting in general case work, it is inevitable that some discussion of basic case work concepts will be included. But in so far as possible, our attention will be focused upon interviewing *per se*. We shall avoid discussing case work concepts as such because case work deserves a much more comprehensive treatment than would be possible here.

The general discussion of the methods and techniques of interviewing, though illustrated at each point, is supplemented by a section giving a number of interviews in more detail. These are annotated by the comments of the author, but they should also provide useful source material on which the experienced interviewer will wish to test his own procedures.

It should be clear that the discussion here presented gives but a selection of some of the most salient features of interviewing. These are culled from a vast store of relevant knowledge accumulated over the years by professional workers in the case work field. Again, it should be noted that there is nothing sacrosanct in the order in which the various topics are treated. They are so inter-related that a discussion of any one of them involves some aspects of many of the others. In practice, things have to be said in a linear order rather than all at once, but it might well be remembered that an understanding of some of the topics treated later will help toward understanding the subjects discussed first.

II.

UNDERSTANDING HUMAN NATURE

THERE are certain basic facts about the nature of human beings with which every interviewer should be familiar. The different motives of interviewers will lead to different uses of such knowledge. The salesman, dominated by the profit motive, will use his knowledge of human psychology to increase his sales; the propagandist, whether his motives are good or bad, will use his knowledge to increase the infectiousness of his ideas. It is assumed that the users of this book will be motivated by the desire to be of service to their fellow human beings and will use their knowledge of human nature to that end.

Human Motivation

The reasons underlying some forms of human behavior are obvious both to the actor and to outside observers. Sometimes they are concealed from outsiders but are recognized more or less clearly by the actor. Sometimes they are unknown even to him. For example, a man applying for a job insults his prospective employer. How can such behavior be understood? Did he not know he was being insulting? Or didn't he know that an insult would prevent his being hired? Or didn't he really want the job? Or what? In seeking to explain his failure to get the job, he might say, "The foreman was unreasonable." But very likely he would himself be aware of the unsatisfactoriness of such an explanation. Often people who behave in some such irrational way as this are as much puzzled by their behavior as is anyone else.

We can sympathize more readily with such a person's bewilderment if we realize that there is much of our own behavior we find hard to explain. Our glib rationalizations do not satisfy even ourselves. Why do we sometimes fly into a rage if we are kept waiting for a minute when at other times we'll wait in line fairly patiently for half an hour? Why do we sometimes punish a child severely for a slight fault and at other times let more severe misbehavior go unremarked? Why do some people in particular "get our goats"?

If we knew all, we would doubtless understand all. Bizarre behavior, like more usual behavior, has its causes, but sometimes they are deeply hidden. In dealing with others it is seldom possible or essential to understand fully the causes of their actions. It is essential, however,

12

to realize that their behavior is motivated. Its source may lie hidden in the depths of their personalities where neither they nor we can readily discover it. In a complex personality with its many interconnected causal chains, the factors underlying a given bit of behavior are usually many and varied. A single cause cannot be isolated, and to attempt to force the individual to name one is to demand the impossible. He will be forced to resort to an inadequate rationalization.

The recognition that much human motivation is unconscious will enable the interviewer to be more tolerant, less condemnatory, and thus better able to help his client effectively. Instead of becoming impatient with rationalizations, he will realize that motives which the client disguises even to himself are probably sources of deep and painful anxiety to him.

Unconscious motivation is much more common than we ordinarily recognize in our attempt to understand people. We seek too often for intellectual *grounds* for behavior rather than for psychological *causes* rooted in feelings and emotions. "Drives" are emotional affairs, and actions controlled by them have their source in feeling rather than in intellect. A person who apparently likes, but really dislikes, another "forgets" a luncheon engagement with him, and in extenuation pleads a busy day. A man fired from a job because of incompetence "explains" that the work was too heavy for him. Why a client says certain things and leaves others unsaid, why a child with a high I.Q. flunks in school, why a wife who effusively protests her love for her husband continually belittles him, are questions whose answers are to be sought not in intellectual but emotional terms. Explanations such as, "He's deceitful," "He's lazy," "She's just being modest about him," are obviously inadequate. Yet for many people such remarks conclude the discussion and block any real understanding.

Objective and Subjective Facts

Every situation has its objective and subjective aspects. A man loses his job. That is an objective fact. His feelings about this event constitute a subjective fact. A man is ill with tuberculosis. That is a medical fact. But every person who has any sort of illness has accompanying it certain feelings about the illness. There are variations in the physical aspects of tuberculosis, but there are many more variations in human reactions to that disease. So we could run the gamut of human experiences and note that every objective experience—marriage, hunger, getting a job, leaving one's children in a day nursery—has its accompanying subjective counterpart of emotional attitudes. Experience and skill lead to more and more awareness of this inter-relationship.

Social workers sometimes contrast what they call the "reality situation" of a client with his emotional problems. This separation is unfortunate because it sometimes leads us to operate as if these two areas were mutually exclusive. The implication is that the emotional components of the situation are not real, whereas, of course, they certainly are real to the person experiencing them. The way one feels about a situation is as much a fact as the situation itself. To avoid such erroneous implications, we shall, in this discussion, speak instead of the objective aspects and the subjective aspects of a client's situation. Both are always present.

If we seem in our discussion to be directing our attention primarily to subjective aspects, to feelings, attitudes, and emotions, this is because we recognize that they are as important as the objective facts themselves and are much more likely to be overlooked. Our concentration upon them does not imply any lack of appreciation of the significance of the objective facts. We recognize, of course, that over-attention to subjective factors would limit our service to the individual just as much as would lack of appreciation of them. In practice we must be extremely vigilant to give each group of factors its due weight.

A student who applies for a scholarship on the grounds that his father has just retired and is unable to see his son through college may be even more worried over his father's poor health, which necessitated the retirement, than he is over the financial problem. The dean who notes only the latter may be failing to give the boy the help he most urgently needs, or may be giving a scholarship to a boy whose anxieties will prevent his profiting from it.

In seeking to help people even in very simple situations we need to listen not only to their objective requests but also to the undertones which reveal their feelings and give us clues as to perhaps even more serious objective situations not overtly revealed. A man's frequent absences from work may indicate neither unreliability nor laziness but may be due to worry about his wife's illness or to anxiety about pressing debts. In either case the underlying subjective factor, worry, is caused by an objective situation which may not be apparent at once to a personnel manager.

Knowledge of subjective factors may be necessary to make possible the formulation of objective plans with some probability that they will be carried out. A worker at the Travelers Aid desk, returning runaway

Mary to her mother in the Middle West, knows that unless she talks to Mary long enough to find out her subjective attitude toward returning home, Mary may get off the bus at the next stop and foil the worker's plan for her safe return.

Moral Pigeonholing

In addition to recognizing the difference between objective and subjective facts, the interviewer should recognize the futility and even danger involved in passing judgment on people's attitudes. Although a mile may seem short to you, to tell a woman who has laboriously walked that distance that she shouldn't feel tired is useless, to say the least. To tell an emotionally upset person that he should be calm may succeed only in erecting a barrier against further expression of his difficulties.

The thermometer of a room may read 72, but the room may feel hot to some and cold to others. A statement about the temperature can be objectively verified or disproved, but to argue about the heat of the room is futile. Disagreement in such a case reflects only differences in subjective feelings, and in so far as one reports these sincerely, one is reporting correctly.

Although we can judge statements about objectively verifiable matters to be true or false, we are not similarly justified in passing judgments on subjective attitudes. Of two people waiting in line, one may sincerely feel the delay to be an imposition, while the other with equal sincerity may regard it as a matter of course. The requirements for eligibility for relief in a given agency may be objectively fixed, but to one client they may seem to involve an unwarranted intrusion into his personal affairs, while to another they may seem to represent only a wise, business-like investigation. One pregnant wife may regard army regulations on leaves as thoroughly exasperating, another as reasonably lenient. One applicant for a job may feel that the interviewer is nosing into his private affairs, another, confronted by the same inquiries, may wonder why more information is not desired. Not the passing of judgment as to the rightness or wrongness of such diverse attitudes but the understanding of their causes should be the aim of the interviewer, for only the latter will be helpful to him in dealing with the situation.

In another area, too, there is a natural but unjustified tendency to judge actions right or wrong. For example, divorce is absolutely taboo in some groups, whereas in others it is expected to occur with a certain normal frequency. A "Down-East Yankee" would rather starve than borrow, but the average American, converted to installment buying, will purchase an auto with no down payment save his old car. But each group tends to regard its own views as absolutely correct, the one condemning divorce or borrowing as absolutely wrong, the other holding that in certain cases, at least, it is completely justifiable. Even legal attitudes change. At one period the sale of alcoholic beverages is a crime and at another a legal business enterprise. Social customs and laws change and people alter their judgments of approval or condemnation.

It is essential for an interviewer to refrain from trying to impose his own moral judgments upon his clients. They should be allowed to discuss their feelings about pertinent matters without fear of condemnation. Knowedge of the flux of social attitudes on even basic ethical matters will tend to make an interviewer less absolute in his judgments of behavior. It would often be desirable if he could refrain from making such judgments about his clients, but—since interviewers, too, are human—he may find this godlike wisdom unattainable and discover that he does have strong feelings of condemnation toward some of their attitudes or behavior. Even where this is the case, however, the good interviewer will learn quickly that any expression of such feelings blocks the progress of the interview. If his interest is genuinely centered in the client, he will learn to keep his own feelings in the background, out of harm's way.

Wisdom will warn the interviewer also against hasty generalizations. He may tend not to trust in any matter a client who lies about his income and may regard as unreliable in other respects as well a youth who lies about his age in order to get a job. This all-or-none attitude permeates everyday thinking. People are regarded as all good or all bad, situations as completely right or thoroughly wrong. Such rigid classifications must be avoided by the interviewer who wishes to understand his client. He must recognize that there are shades and variations of rightness and wrongness. A person who lies about one subject may not lie at all about another. He may be so in need of a job that he'll prevaricate no end to get one, but he may be scrupulously honest about financial matters. People who have fallen into "bad" modes of behavior in one field may be unusually "upright" in others.

"There is so much good in the worst of us, and so much bad in the best of us, that it ill behooves any one of us to find any fault with the rest of us." The truth of this saying is so obvious that we can be sure that any judgment utterly condemning another person will be mistaken. The all-or-none principle fails. But, on the other hand, it is probably a mistake to try to assess accurately just the respects in which a client is good and just the ones in which he is bad. It is much more important to understand him, and to seek the causes of his behavior, even when it is anti-social, than it is to grow indignant about it.

Conflicting Pulls

From birth on we have to make one choice after another. Some choices are relatively easy. In other cases we want very much to have our cake and eat it too. When forced to decide, we do so with much hesitation and often look back on our selection with some misgiving, wondering if we have really chosen wisely. The student who gives up his fraternity beer party to study for an important examination feels the pull of the party very strongly while he tries to study. Sometimes the pull is so strong he reverses his choice and goes to the party, only then to feel the "voice of conscience" striving in vain to pull him back to his work.

In many cases we resolutely put the thought of what we have rejected out of our mind—that is, our conscious mind. But the pull of what we have denied ourselves nevertheless remains and sometimes takes its revenge in devious ways. When a choice has been hard, we cannot deny the attractiveness of what we rejected merely by saying we don't want it. We do want it. What is true is only that under the circumstances we want it less than that which we have chosen. We want to lie abed in the morning, but we want to keep our jobs more. We want to keep slender, but we also want to nibble sweets, and no matter which desire finally has its way with us, the defeated one is likely to rebel now and again.

Although some of us make up our minds more easily than others, we all experience many conflicting interests, desires, and emotions. The harboring of such conflicting feelings is technically known as ambivalence. An understanding of this concept is essential to anyone who is attempting to work successfully with people.

Sometimes an early conflict that was hard to resolve leaves us ambivalent about our choice long after the influences that led us to want what we rejected have ceased to exist. In such cases, our ambivalence is not only unconscious but irrational as well. Nevertheless it exists and has its adequate causes and its effects. Anyone who would understand our behavior today will do so more adequately if he at least knows in general of the existence of unconscious and irrational ambivalence even though he may not know the details of our own case.

One common manifestation of ambivalence occurs in the areas of dependence and independence. Children want to grow up and have the privileges of adults—to smoke cigarettes, to stay up late, and so on. At the same time they want to remain children—to play all day and to be free from responsibilities. This often carries into adulthood so that even with chronological maturity many infantile desires continue to operate. Childhood food fads persist unchecked by adult knowledge. A man may marry primarily (though perhaps unconsciously) for mothering. It is only when the satisfactions of fulfilling adult responsibilities and obtaining adult privileges outweigh the desire for childhood pleasures that the individual grows up emotionally. All of us need to be loved, but for some of us this causes conflict. We fear that accepting love will entail losing some of our cherished independence.

Superficial signs of dependence and independence are sometimes misleading. Here again we need to distinguish between objective and subjective facts. A man may be self-sufficient, an executive, and still subjectively be weighed down by a longing for dependence, thus using up more emotional energy than is necessary day after day in his efforts to maintain himself in his own eyes as an independent adult.

Women want equality with men. They want to work at the same occupations and draw the same salaries as men. But they also want men chivalrously to give up their seats in the subway.

Instances of ambivalence arise continually in interviewing. They are manifested by clients who obviously want help but are unable to ask for it, who ask advice but do not utilize it, who agree to certain plans but do not carry them out, who say one thing but by their behavior indicate the opposite.

The Relationship Between Interviewer and Interviewee

Parents are often amused at the enthusiasm their young son shows for his school teacher. He reports her comments on the weather, imitates her mannerisms, wants to take her gifts, is delighted if she asks him to clean the blackboard for her after school, and so on. Another parent whose child has the same teacher may not understand why he seems negativistic toward all the teacher's suggestions, and seems to go out of his way to annoy and irritate the teacher. Similarly adults themselves, when they stop to think about it, find that their rather strong attachments or antagonisms for certain people seem unjustified by any conscious knowledge they have of the other's nature. Such positive and negative feelings toward those we come in contact with are, of course, universal phenomena, always present to some degree. Certain features of interviewing tend to intensify them, and for this reason the wise interviewer will want to understand their nature and effects and will seek to subject them to some measure of self-conscious control.

For many a client it is a unique experience to talk with someone who, instead of criticizing or admonishing, listens with non-judgmental understanding. This relationship with a person who does not ask anything for himself personally but focuses his interest entirely on the client and yet refrains from imposing advice or control is a very satisfying one. The discovery of these characteristics in the interviewer accompanied as it is by the absence of closer knowledge of the interviewer's personality with its inevitable personal whims and foibles leads the client to idealize him. The client's feelings are unchecked by personal knowledge of the interviewer which might dilute them. He thus endows the worker with the ideal characteristics one is always searching for, quite independently of whether or not the worker actually is such an ideal person.

These feelings are usually not consciously revealed but indications of them may be recognized in such comments from clients as, "It's been such a help to talk with you," "I see you understand," "You're the first person I've ever told this to," "What do you think I should do?" Remarks of this sort occur in case after case.

The opposite sort of situation also arises in interviewing. Again quite independently of the interviewer's actual character, the client, because of his own anxieties, insecurity, and deprivations, may endow him with negative characteristics and build up antagonism toward him. Much depends on the client's previous experiences with his parents or with others in authority.

Negative feelings are often even more concealed than positive ones because of social standards of politeness, but they are revealed sometimes by refusals to talk, by the breaking off of an appointment, by refusal to return to the agency, or by trapping the worker into giving advice which can later be proved wrong.

The development of excessive negative or positive feelings by the client is often alarming to the interviewer who may be unaware of having done anything to arouse such feelings. An interviewer tends to want his clients to like him, but sometimes in his eagerness to achieve this end he unwittingly encourages more dependency than he had realized was potentially present. A worker should realize that the development of an emotional rapport, positive or negative, between the client and himself is not abnormal but inevitable, and that he should direct his attention not to eliminating this relationship but to controlling its nature and intensity. He must guard against misleading the client into an overly dependent relationship through appearing too personally friendly or appearing to promise too much, but on the other hand he must not lean over backward in avoiding this danger and make the client feel that he is an unresponsive and unsympathetic listener. It is easy, when one is treated like God, to assume the characteristics of that role, and it is easy to over-correct this tendency.

If an interviewer notices that the relationship with his client seems to be developing negatively, he should not become overly alarmed because this may be due not at all to him but to factors deeply hidden in his client's personality. He should review his own activity in the case and make sure that he has given no objective grounds for the antagonism the client seems to feel for him. He may have given inadequate help, broken an appointment, or himself have developed negative feelings toward the client of which he was not fully aware. If there are no such objective sources for his client's negativism, he can assure the client by a continued attempt to understand the reasons for his difficulties that he is not retaliating with disapproval of his own.

The development of an inter-relationship of this general sort, positive or negative, between interviewer and interviewee is not at all a unique phenomenon but a universal one. It is a commonplace that people tend to become dependent upon their doctors, lawyers, and ministers. Toward the end of her pregnancy a woman often relies more on her physician than on her husband. A patient under psychoanalysis develops a strong emotional attachment to the analyst. The analyst has developed methods of making therapeutic use of such a relationship. He calls it technically "transference." We are concerned with it here only in some of the less intense forms mentioned above.

III.

THE INTERVIEWER'S ATTITUDES

THE importance of the interviewer's attitudes will have become clear by now. It is impossible to discuss the interviewee's attitudes and the conduct of an interview without commenting on the interviewer's attitudes at every point. All the things said about understanding human beings apply also to the interviewer, for he too is a human being, with unconscious as well as conscious motivation, ambivalence, prejudices, and objective and subjective reasons for his behavior. He brings to his relationship with the interviewee his own predetermined attitudes, which may profoundly affect that relationship. He has a natural tendency to impute to others his own feelings and may thus seriously misunderstand his client's situation and problem. If he is unable to bear frustration or poverty, he may find it difficult to comprehend his client's toleration of it. An interviewer who finds it difficult to reveal himself to others may decide that a client should not be "probed," when as a matter of fact the client wants nothing so much as to be helped to talk. We now discuss two of the many specific respects in which the interviewer needs to be particularly aware of his own feelings in order to be able to help the client satisfactorily.

Prejudices

Most of us often remark the prejudices of others but seldom are conscious of our own, for in our own case we regard them as natural opinions. When we are irritated or enthusiastic, when we react with anger, disgust, shame, pride, or love, it seems as if such situations would naturally cause such feelings in any normal person. A helpful step in discovering our own prejudices is to jot down a list of those we know others to possess. A little self-scrutiny will then convince us that these are not as alien to our own attitudes as we may have assumed.

We usually think of prejudices as large over-all attitudes such as race prejudice, class prejudice, religious, or political prejudice. Here we are concerned rather with much smaller matters, subtler and more easily escaping notice. We find exaggerated dislikes of sloppy dressers, flashy dressers, skinny people, fat people, show-offs, weak men, aggressive women, blondes, brunettes, or redheads. Elsewhere we find exaggerated fondness for blondes, brunettes, or redheads, arrow-collared

Tarzans, pipe-smokers, women with slender ankles, or men with curly hair. Some interviewers prefer rather self-sufficient clients who state their cases incisively; others prefer meek clients who need considerable help to express their needs; few can avoid responding with warm satisfaction to "grateful" clients.

A comparison of our own list of prejudices with those of others will reveal the great variety in different individuals' attitudes toward the same sort of occurrence. For example, everyone has distinct ideas of his own as to what is really intolerable. Some can easily tolerate and attempt to understand the alcoholic but find a lazy person intolerable. For another laziness stirs no personal emotion but lying is an unpardonable sin. "I don't care what a person does so long as he is honest. I cannot bear to be deceived." Again, for others, even the most involved deception is passed over as a "white lie" but poor housekeeping is beyond the pale. A few find murder more easily acceptable than procrastination. In so far as an interviewer can discover his own areas of intolerance, his own list of unpardonable sins, he has made a start toward self-disciplined control of his feelings in his relationships with others.

When an interviewer first learns that he should be non-judgmental, should not become angry, should not become dependent upon the interviewee's affection and response, he tries to suppress his feelings, and as a result he tends to become artificial and stilted in his responses. It would be better to recognize the existence of such feelings and learn to control their expression, for these feelings are not unnatural but merely inappropriate in the professional situation. If an interviewer is aware that he is becoming angry, he is then in a position to regulate his own feelings better than if he denies to himself that he has such feelings. Control of feelings rather than absence of feelings on the part of the worker is the goal.

Acceptance

We have spoken of the value of tolerance in an interviewer. But it is not easy to say how an interviewer can accept aberrant behavior or attitudes on the part of a client and yet maintain his own and the community's standards. Interviewers sometimes learn that they should be "accepting" without knowing very clearly what is involved in acceptance. Knowing the word gives them a false assurance that they understand its significance.

In the training of the individual certain standards of behavior are inevitably imposed, first by parents and later by society. It is natural that the individual in learning to condemn his own unacceptable behavior should include in his condemnation similar behavior on the part of others. If, for example, he has learned to be neat, he tends to abhor slovenliness in others. The interviewer must learn to counteract this perfectly natural tendency to condemn all behavior that conflicts with his own standards. Toward almost every problem that a client brings, the interviewer has developed an attitude of approval or disapproval based on his own experiences, and he tends to assume that this attitude represents the norm. As his professional training and experience grow he recognizes that there is a wide range of individual variation in human responses to a given situation. This may lead him to try to accept all such behavior, to carefully refrain from evaluating it. But this clearly is an extremely limited understanding of the concept of acceptance, involving as it does only an arid non-judgmental impartiality. Real acceptance is primarily acceptance of the feelings given expression by behavior and does not necessarily involve acceptance of unsocial behavior at all; real acceptance involves positive and active understanding of these feelings and not merely a negative and passive refusal to pass judgment.

A merely negative attitude of not passing judgment on a client's unusual behavior is often interpreted by him as a condoning of that behavior, a repudiation of a standard he himself accepts but has failed to live up to. He tends then either to reject the interviewer as an unfit guide or at the other extreme to continue and increase his undesirable behavior thus trying out the interviewer to see how far he can go in his nonconformity. A man who makes no effort to get a job, for instance, may find his dilatoriness so accepted by the interviewer that he gradually gives up the struggle for self-maintenance entirely. A child whose petty stealing is ignored is not at all reassured, as he would be if he were confronted by the interviewer with knowledge of this misbehavior and yet convinced that in spite of this the worker accepted him in the fuller sense of understanding his feelings and the emotional conflicts which induced his stealing. A child feels that a person who thus understands him is his friend. Such a person's recognition of misbehavior will be regarded as a sign that he wants to help overcome it.

To accept then is not to condone anti-social behavior but to understand it in the sense of understanding the feelings it expresses. In a worker's early acquaintance with a client it is of course impossible to know, let alone understand specifically, all of the various factors responsible for given behavior. In such early stages we make use of the best knowledge we have available at that time, namely, the general familiarity we have acquired through theory and experience with the basic underlying dynamics of human behavior. We know that a person who appears angry and belligerent may, in fact, be feeling anxious and fearful, that one who appears demanding may have no other way to express his hurt pride and guilt about asking advice or aid. Understanding of this sort lays the groundwork for real acceptance. As an interviewer's knowledge of the client deepens, however, his general knowledge is enlarged by an understanding of the particular pressures active in this specific situation. His general acceptance develops into more specific understanding. Such detailed understanding is not always possible, but the more definite it is the more effective the worker can be.

Sometimes an interviewer, relying on his general understanding, says too readily, "I understand," and thus confuses and blocks the client in his attempt to present the details that would be needed for more specific understanding. The interviewer means that he wants to understand, or does understand in general, whereas the client realizes that he certainly does not yet know about the specific factors of his case. It often would be far better for the interviewer to say, "I do not understand," for then the client would realize that the interviewer wants to understand but needs more information.

Another easy error is to offer false reassurances. "I'm sure you'll soon be well." "I know you'll get a job soon." "Everything will be all right." Such remarks, far from reassuring the client, usually cause him rather to doubt the worker's understanding of the situation and consequently his ability to help. It would be more judicious and also more helpful to be realistic about the situation, to offer hope only where there is good ground for it. The interviewer's recognition of the client's own doubts can itself be reassuring, for the client feels that he has in the interviewer someone who knows the worst and yet will still help him.

In the relationship between interviewer and interviewee, intellectual understanding is clearly insufficient unless it is accompanied by emotional understanding as well. Intellectual knowledge may suffice for mathematics or logic, but to understand intellectually the successive movements of dancing or skiing does not qualify one as a good dancer or skier. Similarly, in our relationships with other human beings, intellectual understanding is barren unless accompanied by emotional understanding. To know about emotions and feelings is not enough. One should be able to "sense" their existence and their degree and quality. Such ability does not come merely from reading a book such as this or merely from classroom study but requires the constant application of theoretical knowledge in practical day-to-day contact with human beings and their objective and subjective problems.

IV.

PURPOSES OF INTERVIEWING

T HE method of conducting an interview will be influenced to a considerable extent by the purpose of that interview. As we have already noted, some interviews are directed primarily to obtaining information, some primarily to giving help, but most involve a combination of the two. The aim is to obtain knowledge of the problem to be solved and sufficient understanding of the person troubled and of the situation so that the problem can be solved effectively. Whether these two functions of understanding and helping are combined in one agency or interviewer or divided among several will modify the detail of the methods used but not their essentials.

One early caution is worth noting. The interviewer is sometimes so anxious to help that he rushes ahead without first obtaining a sound understanding of the situation. That such a procedure can be destructive rather than helpful should be clear. To advise a boy to continue in high school without first obtaining knowledge of his interests and abilities is obviously unwise. The first and basic purpose of interviewing is to obtain understanding of the problem, of the situation, and of the client who has come for help.

Another caution to be kept in mind throughout is that although the interviewer should be clearly aware of his purposes it is not always wise to seek to realize them by direct action. Even where considerable information is desired, it is often best obtained by encouraging the client to talk freely of his problem rather than by asking such pointed questions as, "Were you fired from your last job?" People are sensitive about their personal life, family skeletons, poverty, past mistakes, and so on, and early flat-footed inquiry may only alienate a client and cause him to erect protective barriers against what may well seem to him unwarranted intrusion. Once convinced of the worker's sensitive understanding, of his desire to know not out of wanton curiosity but only in order to help, and of the confidential nature of the relationship, the client will welcome an opportunity to talk about things which earlier he would have suppressed.

The specific kinds of help an interviewer can give, and consequently the specific sort of information he will seek, is determined to a considerable extent by the functions of his agency. He may want to obtain the kind of information that will be needed to give medical aid, or the kind needed for relief or child-placing, or employment, and so on. Within this general field, he will be guided by the indications his client gives him of the special facts involved in this particular case. He will first listen to his client's statement of his needs and then guide the interview along those channels which seem most appropriate to the specific circumstances of this case. A good general alters his strategy for reaching a given goal according to changes in the situation, and a good interviewer will modify his techniques as circumstances demand.

The information to be sought by an interviewer is sometimes fixed in advance by a printed form or specific instructions from the interviewer's superior. In such cases it is essential that the interviewer be thoroughly acquainted with the purposes back of each question and understand its significance. Otherwise he tends to ask the questions in a perfunctory manner that minimizes their importance to the interviewee and raises doubts as to the significance of the interview. Further, an interviewer is inclined to accept superficial and inadequate answers to questions whose purport he has not grasped. Unless he understands the purpose of obtaining certain information or carrying out certain plans for the client, he will frequently be unable to do either effectively.

For example, an interviewer asked simply to obtain a developmental history of a sick sailor may do so in a perfunctory manner which will miss many significant details. If, however, he knows some of the ways in which a psychiatrist may use such information in helping a man who has had a sudden "breakdown," he will be able to do a much more adequate job.

Again, a case worker must frequently carry out policies with which he is not in accord, for example, administer what he regards as an inadequate budget, but his own lack of conviction will interfere less if he is fully conscious of it.

The interviewee, too, should be helped to feel that each question is important and significant. In addition to the presence of this conviction on the part of the interviewer, it may be necessary to explain in a way that will satisfy the interviewee the relevance of the questions to his own needs and interests. A question as to one's birthplace may seem irrelevant until one realizes its importance in determining citizenship. A question as to what floor the client lives on assumes more significance in a heart case; questions about diet are called for in tuberculosis cases; early developmental history has special significance in children's behavior problems; the number of jobs held in the past ten years is important in gauging a man's employability.

Every interview has, to begin with, its manifest purpose. If an agency has initiated an interview and called someone in, the person interviewed can usually be put most quickly at his ease—relieved of uncertainty in the face of the unknown—and the interview most quickly advanced, by a straightforward statement in terms the client can readily grasp of the interviewer's purpose in asking him to come in for a consultation. Where the interviewee asks for the appointment, the situation is a little different. In such cases, rather than greet him with a barrage of questions, it is better to let him state in his own words his problem and his purpose in coming in for an interview. Sometimes the client is nervous and incoherent, but he is most quickly reassured if he is allowed to begin the interview in his own way. Often the interviewer can learn much from the very hesitancy and indirect way in which the client approaches the account of his difficulty.

The worker will of course keep in mind the specific functions of his agency, as these sometimes delimit rather sharply the area in which he can be of service. Sometimes he can help most by referring the client to some other agency whose ability to aid will be more pertinent to his needs. Ordinarily, however, even this should not be done immediately, for often the manifest purpose of the client differs considerably from his real purpose, and the latter may well fall within the field of the given agency or require reference to a quite different agency from the one that first comes to the interviewer's mind. A woman with three children applying for a job may need first of all an opportunity to clarify her own thoughts as to whether she wants to work and place her children or whether she wants to seek financial assistance from a relief agency in order to maintain her home. Only after this question has been settled can we know where to refer her.

Most people who come seeking help or advice are considerably troubled by their problem, as is evidenced by the fact that their anxieties have risen to such a pitch as to drive them to take the step of seeking this consultation. This anxiety may make it difficult for them to see their problem distinctly or state it clearly. Very often their problem will be so involved that they are unable to come anywhere near locating the root of the trouble. A man who comes in to register for a job may really need medical attention. A woman who is anxious about the development of her children may have more real need to

28

discuss with someone her troubled relationship with her husband. And so on.

An inexperienced interviewer will always keep in mind the possibility that his client is suffering from some trouble more difficult than he realizes or is able to state. He will endeavor by various methods to put his client at ease, to stimulate him to talk relatively freely about his problem, and to help him to organize his own confused thoughts and feelings about his difficulties. Sometimes talking about the situation to a sympathetic listener will itself lead to a satisfactory conclusion. The client's thoughts may thus be organized so clearly that he sees himself what action he should take. His fears and hesitancies may be removed and he may be encouraged to take whatever action is necessary. More often, perhaps, just talking is not enough and help of other sorts will be required. We shall discuss some of these things later. Our purpose now is to call attention to the desirability of looking beyond manifest purposes to more fundamental latent ones that may be present.

It is of course possible to probe too far. Some sleeping dogs should be left undisturbed. This is particularly true when the interviewer is not equipped to deal with them should they be aroused. Even a skilled interviewer should use a good deal of discretion and wisdom in going beneath the surface.

The fact that interviews bring to light new knowledge of purposes and needs as well as new information about the relevant facts implies that the interviewer should not let his plan of action be unalterably fixed in advance or determined early in the interview. A certain amount of flexibility is always desirable.

V.

HOW TO INTERVIEW

ALTHOUGH the most skilful interviewing gives the appearance of being a smooth and spontaneous interchange between the interviewer and the interviewee, the skill thus revealed is obtained only through careful study and years of practice. For purposes of study it is possible to break down an interview into a number of component factors and discuss each separately. In actual interviewing, of course, no such sharp breaks occur, but we must make them in analysis if our discussion is not to be so general as to be relatively valueless. The interviewer must become conscious of the various subtleties in interviewing before he can absorb them into his spontaneous responses. First recognized in theory, they later become so much a part of the worker's skill that they are utilized naturally at each step without conscious notice. We hear much of the intuitive skill of the trained interviewer. But back of such skill lies much study of the various processes and interrelationships involved in interviewing. The skilful skier is unconscious of the many movements integrated in his smooth flight, but earlier he had to learn them painfully one by one and then learn to combine them into a harmonious co-ordinated whole.

One danger that arises from an analytical treatment such as we must necessarily undertake is that an interviewer, in his attempt to find a few simple rules that will guide him, will seize upon certain techniques which are highly valuable in certain cases and apply them in others where they are less relevant. Supervisors notice that words of a case worker, reported in a case and discussed favorably in staff meeting, begin to recur time and again in the reports of her young students. We should remember that each technique suggested has its limitations and should be used only on appropriate occasions and in conjunction with other techniques which are equally demanded by the whole situation. In practice none of the methods to be discussed operates in a vacuum but only in organic relation with most of the others.

Observation

In one sense all that we shall say about interviewing might well come under the head of observation. Here we shall discuss a few of the simpler and more obvious types of observation important in all interviewing. It goes almost without saying that we should observe what the interviewee says. It is less obvious to remark that we should note equally what he does not say, what significant gaps there are in his story. We should note also such things as bodily tensions, flushing, excitability, and dejection, because they supplement, and sometimes even belie, the picture given by the client's words. The following opening sentences of the report of an interview reveal how much is told by the physical behavior of the client.

Mrs. Marsh comes into the office and asks for temporary aid. We notice her sitting in the waiting-room before our interview with her, sitting in a very erect posture, almost rigidly, clenching her hands in her lap. Her face is very white and drawn. When she comes into the interviewing room she is so tense and nervous that she can hardly talk; and as she sits rigidly in her chair looking directly at the worker, she wrings her hands. She is a large, well-built woman, with very light, coarse hair, extremely blue eyes, and a fair skin. She has what looks to be an extremely severe case of acne, which mars her complexion. When we ask Mrs. Marsh to tell us how we may help her, she speaks in short, jerky sentences, giving her story with no logical sequence.

Out of all the things to be observed, each interviewer will remark only a relatively small number. His selection will be determined by his own observational equipment as limited by his interests, prejudices, attitudes, and training. Since it seems impossible to make note of things without adding a personal element of interpretation, he may even modify considerably in his own picture of the situation the data actually presented to him. To illustrate this influence of the observer's own nature on his reports the following experiment is sometimes conducted in an early session of a case work class.

Students are asked to write in not more than a page an observation they have made of an individual or a group of individuals. The observation may take place in a restaurant, at a railroad station, on the street, or on the campus. Students are asked to perform this experiment in pairs; two students observe the same scene and write it up without comparing notes. These parallel papers are then read in class. Such a project is unusually convincing in illustrating the subjective variations of the observer. Sometimes the write-ups are so different that the students cannot believe they are of the same situation. In one an individual is described as angry, callous to the pleas of his child for an ice-cream cone. In the other he is reported as anxious, uncertain, indecisive, frustrated, and helpless in the face of a demanding offspring in a temper tantrum. A project of this sort directs a student's attention to the limi-

31

tations of his own capacity to see what is actually happening and to his tendency to distort the objective facts with his own preconceived ideas of what he himself would feel or do in such a situation.

That we cannot take for granted that our observation of an individual is accurate is initially a blow to our self-confidence. It is a blow, however, that may help to break down any preconceived ideas about our infallibility and pave the way to self-scrutiny and the development of a more observant capacity to size up situations as they really are. It comes at first as a surprise that what seems like anger to one person may be sensed as anxiety by another. What seems like cocky self-assurance to one may be sensed as tense insecurity by another. What seems like "sweetness and light" to one may be recognized as hostility by another. Such differences in interpretation arise partly from the facts that people do not always behave and act as they feel, that they do not always say what they really mean, and that they do not always behave logically and rationally. But in part they are due to the fact that everyone necessarily looks at the rest of the world from his own immediate point of view, which always seems to him the natural, logical, sensible one. When an interviewer realizes that a client's point of reference seems like the reasonable one to him, it becomes clear that it is important to attempt to understand how the situation looks from his viewpoint and why that seems to him to be the only correct way of looking at things. If we attempt to do this before trying to persuade him to what seems to us a more logical point of view, we have made a faint beginning of understanding him.

Many times a client finds in the interviewer the first person in his experience who can listen understandingly and yet not intrude upon his feelings or attempt to redirect his behavior. This experience for the client is sometimes surprisingly satisfying. As just noted, it alone is sometimes helpful. At other times it is merely one part of a helping process.

That people do not always say what they mean or act as they feel is continually apparent in interviewing. For example, case workers in relief agencies repeatedly have the experience of having a client storm into the office belligerently demanding immediate financial support, only to have him reveal when met with kindness that underneath he is really frightened, ashamed of his poverty, and pleading for understanding of the mess in which he finds himself.

Another illustration of the value of observing more than appears on the surface is afforded by the following interview from a Travelers Aid desk.

"You've got to get me to New York." A man in seaman's uniform was standing by the desk glaring belligerently at me. He had been drinking. He was so angry he was sputtering. "They put me off the train here because I didn't have a ticket — they don't do things like that in England." We asked him what they did in England. In England they just take your name and address and let you travel through, then the railroad solicitor writes you a letter asking for the fare. We said we could see how he felt about this and we thought we could help him if he could tell us a little more about how he happened to be put off the train.

He became calmer with the assurance that something would be done and said with a decided English accent, "I'm a British seaman — I've ferried American soldiers across. I went to Philadelphia yesterday to see the city because I heard it was interesting. I had a little drink in me and I must have lost my ticket, because I couldn't find it when the conductor wanted to see it — so they pushed me off here, and I haven't any money nor any relatives in New York City, and I have to be back immediately. You can't get in touch with my steamship because they are not giving out any information. I've got to get there in a hurry."

We asked him for his identification. He said, "I've got all my papers." He showed us his alien registration card and other identifying information. We assured him they were enough and gave him money to buy a ticket to New York. He had some time before the train left which he spent telling us that his wife and child were in England and showed us their pictures and their home, which he would see soon —he hoped. As he left he said, "I am on the S.S. — so if you read about the boat, think of me." We said we would and wished him a safe journey.

Listening

One type of observation occurs through listening. This is one of the fundamental operations of interviewing, and it goes without saying that a good interviewer is a good listener. But what constitutes a good listener? One who frequently interrupts to say what he would have done under similar circumstances is not a good listener, but neither is he who sits like a bump on a log. Absence of response may easily seem to the talker to reflect absence of interest. Everyone knows from his own experience in telling a story that people like a listener who indicates by brief relevant comments or questions that he has grasped the essential points of one's tale, and who adds illuminating comments on certain significant features of one's account that had not been stressed and might well have been overlooked by an inattentive listener. This attention to important details that had not been emphasized gives the story teller the stimulating feeling that the listener not only wants to, but does understand, to an unusual degree, what he is trying to say.

A common error of an inexperienced interviewer is to be embarrassed by silences and to feel that he must fill them with questions or comments. A decent respect for silences is often more helpful. Sometimes the person interviewed falls silent because he is a little reluctant to go on with what comes next in his story, or because he doesn't quite know how to formulate what he plans to say. A too hasty interruption may leave this important part of the story forever unsaid. Sometimes, of course, a silence is due to other causes, and if allowed to continue will only embarrass the person interviewed. In such cases a pertinent remark or question will encourage him to continue.

Listening to a client's story is sometimes helpful in and of itself. Everyone knows the value at times of "letting off steam." When something happens that upsets a person or "makes him mad" he tends to get over these feelings more quickly if he can find a sympathetic friend who will let him "rave" for awhile. Relieved, he can then go ahead and use his energy more constructively. Without this opportunity to talk it out with someone else, he may "boil" for days. He probably does not want anyone to tell him what to do or what he should have done differently, but may merely want someone to listen and understand how upset he is. It is unfortunate that the average lay person is not a good listener. He usually feels impelled to point out the other person's mistakes and faults or give advice about what to do.

The following interview from an employment agency illustrates how valuable mere listening can be.

Mrs. Cobb comes in to register for a job, but there is such difficulty with simple matters such as name, address, former jobs, and so on, and she seems so upset that I say perhaps she feels these details are not important, that possibly we should talk about a definite job for her first. She says that she doesn't mind very much about answering the questions, but that she doesn't know what she would do if she should get a job. I ask how she means this and she says that everything at home is all upset and it keeps her worried all the time. I reply that many people feel they can only talk about employment when they come to this agency, but that we are interested in helping people in every way possible, and that I know there are many things besides a job that can be worrisome. She says that I have "certainly told the truth that time," and proceeds to tell a very long and involved story about many troubles with her husband, children, death in the family, and so on. When she has finished I say that she certainly has had many troubles and that I should like to help her if she feels there is something I can do. She says she thinks she can manage everything by herself, but that today she had been walking all over town just worrying to herself and was "nearly crazy," and felt she just had to talk to somebody. She says that she does not often get this way, but when she does she just has to talk to someone.

After she talks she always feels better, but she feels best when she talks to somebody that knows "what it is all about." I say that we have used up a great deal of time with this, and now there is someone else waiting to see me, but that I should be glad to make an appointment for her to come back to talk either about the job or something else that we may be able to do for her. In preparing to leave she says she does not think it necessary to come back as she thinks that things are going to be better, and that she has a part-time job that helps out with family expenses. She seems much more cheerful than when she came in, and I remark that I am glad we were able to help her even if all we gave her was conversation. She replies that I am still young, and that some day I will learn that "conversation is a wonderful thing."

There is, however, a danger in allowing the client undirected expression of his feelings. They may be due not to a recent upsetting experience but to a long chain of experiences going back into the remote past. These early experiences may have become twisted and distorted and inter-related with other things through the years so that mere talking does not bring relief. His need to talk may not be occasional but constant, and if the interviewer encourages too much release of feeling, areas may be opened up with which both interviewer and client are unequipped to cope. In general, catharsis through talking is more effective the more the disturbing feeling is related to a fairly recent experience, and it becomes of dubious value the more the feeling is due to long repressed experiences. If a difficult situation may be immediately aired, the danger of its being pushed from consciousness but remaining an active source of anxiety is lessened. If a person has had a hairbreadth automobile escape, he feels better if he can talk about it a lot for a while, for then its importance gradually wanes and is forgotten. Particularly with children it is helpful to remember that if they do have a traumatic experience—an accident, an operation, a sex assault—the more immediately they can be helped to express their feelings about it, the less will it be in danger of becoming a source of neurotic conflict. It is as if the wound should be kept open long enough to drain off the infection in order to avoid a festering sore.

A U.S.O. Travelers Aid worker reported the following incident.[1]

A young soldier, asking for information about a place to eat, seemed nervous and upset. He lingered after the worker had given him the information, and she asked him if there was anything further she could help him with. He said there was nothing else, but went on to say that he supposed he had to eat but didn't feel like it. He had been upset since morning when he had lost his

---

[1] "The Scene Shifts for Travelers Aid," by Evelyn Heacox, *The Family,* February, 1942, p. 333.

buddy in a fatal accident during maneuvers. He described in detail how his friend had been run over by a tractor, and went over again and again the gruesome details of the accident he had witnessed. The boys had come from the same state where they had gone to school together. They had entered the army at the same time and had always been inseparable. He seemed to get some relief through talking about it and said, when he left, that he "felt a lot better."

Listening Before Talking
or "Begin Where the Client Is"

The first step in an interview is to help the interviewee relax and feel fairly comfortable. Naturally this is difficult to accomplish unless the interviewer himself is relaxed. Sometimes the client can quickly be put at ease by letting him state his purpose in coming, sometimes by giving him a brief account of why he was asked to come. In either case, an advisable next step is to encourage him to talk, and then to listen carefully while he speaks of what is on the "top" of his mind in connection with the interview. This gives the interviewer a chance to become acquainted with him, to know what language he speaks, literally and figuratively. It makes clear the kind of questions, comments, and suggestions that should later be directed to him and the way in which they should be formulated. It is as unsatisfactory to talk Harvard English with a person used to popular slang as it is to use slang expressions with a professor totally unfamiliar with them.

Even when our primary interest in a given interview is to obtain the answers to a set of questions, we can profit much from letting the client talk rather freely at first. He will usually reveal the answers to many questions without their being asked and often will suggest the best methods of approach for obtaining any additional information that is required.

Where suggestions are to be made by the interviewer it is even more important to let the client express himself first. Sometimes he will even suggest the course of action that the interviewer intends to advise, and in such case his own suggestion can simply be confirmed and strengthened, the fact that he regards it as coming from himself making it more likely that he will carry it out. In other cases the client may reveal a deep-seated hostility to the suggestion about to be made, and in this case the interviewer is warned to proceed with caution and to attempt to discover and remove or modify the emotional causes back of the hostility before proposing his plan.

Another advantage in letting the interviewee talk first is that it tends to counteract any preconceived ideas about him which the interviewer may have allowed himself to entertain. It gives the interviewer the immense advantage of being able to see the situation and the client's problem from the client's point of view. Since it is the client who eventually must act, it is obviously advantageous to start from where he is rather than from some vantage point of the interviewer even though the latter might otherwise be superior.

If someone comes in and asks for a job and the interviewer proceeds at once to make a number of suggestions, he may well be surprised later to find that the client has adopted no one of them. Upon further examination the worker may then find out what he might well have discovered in the first interview if he had done more listening and less talking, that the client's real worry was that he couldn't hold a job if he got one, or that he didn't see how he could take a job because his wife and children were sick at home and needed constant care.

Questioning

Perhaps the central method of interviewing is the fine art of questioning. We shall discuss only a few of its many features.

It may be usual in a police station to ask blustering, bullying questions. It is a common occurrence in a courtroom for a clever attorney to ask tricky questions. But such devices are inappropriate in a case work interview; there cross-examination and the third degree are ruled out. The method of the case work interview is the method of friendliness, the method of asking questions in order to understand and be of assistance. Clients soon recognize the attitudes of their interviewers and tend to respond to the best of their abilities when they feel the presence of a real desire to understand and help.

The interviewer who puts his questions accusingly or suspiciously arouses only fear and suspicion, not co-operation. The wording of the question is often of less importance than the manner and tone of voice in which it is put. The interviewer's safeguard here is really to be interested in understanding and aiding; then his manner and tone are very likely to reflect that interest.

The question, "Are you looking for work?" may sound suspicious, accusing, sarcastic, or friendly, depending upon how it is expressed, and that in turn reflects how the interviewer really feels.

Questioners who are beginning to find out about the influence of unconscious desires and emotions on human behavior sometimes come to enjoy so much the discovery of some hidden motive or influence that they cannot resist letting the client know that they "see through" him.

They experience the joy of the amateur detective, and by revealing this attitude, alienate their client. A more mature understanding would lead them instead to increased sympathy with a person in such distress that he had been forced to conceal important facts even from himself.

A similar error consists in becoming so interested in the mysterious realms of the unconscious that the interviewer probes his client unnecessarily, to satisfy his interest in the esoteric. Though probing for a bullet is pretty painful, mental probing can be far worse, and realization of this should cause an interviewer to carry his inquiry only as far as is necessary for him to be effectively helpful.

A good general rule is to question for only one of two purposes: to obtain specifically needed information, and to direct the client's conversation from fruitless to fruitful channels. Included in the latter would be questions that encourage him to talk in relevant areas where he finds the going difficult, and remarks such as "I don't quite understand," which will help him to elaborate more fully.

Most people tend to ask either too many questions or too few. Each interviewer should study his own tendency and seek to curb it. Too many questions will confuse and block the client, while too few may place too much of the burden of the interview on him and may leave salient areas unexplored.

In general, leading rather than pointed questions, and questions that cannot be answered by a brief "yes" or "no" are to be preferred. They stimulate the client to talk freely and avoid the always present danger of putting answers into his mouth. Even if questions that imply an answer do not result in false answers, they tend to give the impression that the questioner is lacking in fundamental understanding of the situation. "Would $5 be enough?" is not as good a query as, "How much do you need?"

A questioner should of course try to adjust his pace to that of his client. To go too slowly suggests lack of interest or understanding. To push ahead too fast is to miss important clues, to confuse the client, and to suggest in a different way that we are not really interested in what he has to say. Again we must accept the client's pace in the sense of not pushing him to reveal more than he is prepared to at any one time. To ask him to reveal confidences before we have won his confidence is to court defeat.

There are no magical questions we can use on all occasions as the good fairy uses her wand. Sometimes in reading a case record, a student comes across a question that was so timely and effective that he is tempted to use it in his own next interviews and is surprised that it does not bring the same rewarding results.

In general, we seem to get further by being encouraging and sympathetic, by leading the client to talk freely, than by trying to drag information out of him by belaboring him with questions.

Talking

Closely allied to questions are the comments of the interviewer. Sometimes the only difference between the two lies in the speaker's inflection. "You found your last job pretty difficult" is either a query or a comment, depending on whether one raises or lowers the pitch of the last syllables. In any case, both questions and comments are species of talking, and certain rules hold for both. In general, the interviewer should comment only for purposes similar to those for which he asks questions—to reassure or encourage the interviewee, to lead him on to discuss further relevant matters, and so on. The one additional kind of talking that goes beyond these purposes is the definite giving of information or advice. As suggested earlier, this stage should come after the interviewer is familiar enough with the client's situation to know whether suggestions will be acceptable or pertinent.

The National Travelers Aid has issued the following suggestions to its workers in a paragraph entitled, "The Art of Giving Information."[2]

There is a real art in giving information. The volunteers must be interested in giving it. A perfunctory response will keep the inquirer from asking other questions or even from repeating his original question in case he has not understood the answer. A bored expression is obvious to other people nearby which may cause them to decide from the volunteer's manner whether they will avail themselves of her service. A cordial manner, such as one would use in meeting guests, is desirable. In fact, people coming to a T.A.S. desk are in a sense guests of the T.A.S. for the moment. A pleasant, gracious greeting and a pleasant, "May I help you?" will encourage questions while a taciturn, gloomy expression and no word of greeting will repel them.

Written directions, if they are at all complicated, are preferable to those given only verbally but often there is not time to write them. It is always wise to have the person repeat the directions if there is not time to write them out.

The volunteer will soon learn that the first question is often only a "trial balloon" asked while the questioner gathers courage to ask the thing he really wants to know. This is another reason for the friendly inviting impression which the volunteer must make. If the question is asked in a hesitating, halting manner or if the person lingers or if he turns away in an undecided manner, the volunteer has a responsibility to help the questioner by some such remark

---

[2] Work Letter to Travelers Aid Staff Members, October 29, 1941.

as "Is there something else you wish to ask about?" or "Maybe my answer wasn't clear to you." It must be remembered that many of the people who ask questions are not sure of themselves and so may not be direct about their questions. The volunteer must be sure, therefore, that she understands the question as well as that the questioner understands the answer.

There is a great difference between expressing a meaning and communicating a meaning. Since the latter is the aim of the interviewer he must devote considerable care to his manner of expression. He must "think with wisdom" but speak the language of his client, including as far as possible the idiom of the client.

A farmer, seeking a loan on his herd of cows was puzzled by a question as to their "evaluation." When the banker tried to explain by asking "What is the price of them?" he answered, "Oh, they are not for sale." The banker replied, "But if they were for sale what would their price be?" The farmer insisted, "But they are not for sale. I wouldn't think of selling them. I've spent eight years building up that herd."

So often words used by one group are not understood by another. This is obviously true of technical words such as "resources," "siblings," and "eligibility," and the specialized terms of such fields as law, medicine, or psychiatry. But also many everyday terms are used with quite different senses by different people. A person given to exaggeration may describe an event as "catastrophic" which another would call "a slight accident." The difficulty of transmitting meaning is aptly illustrated by questionnaires. How many who have filled out the pesky things have ever understood all the questions? An interviewer who remembers his perplexities on such occasions can readily sympathize with his clients and even anticipate some of their difficulties.

It is not enough that all the words used by the interviewer should be understood; it is important also that they be understood as they were meant. For example, many case workers bandy about such terms as love, hate, anger, and hostility in a rather loose way, meaning to include quite weak emotions as well as strong ones, whereas to many a client anger involves at least such overt phenomena as flushing of the face, clenching of the fists, rapid increase of heartbeat, respiration, and so on. The worker who tells his client, "I know you were angry with me for missing our last appointment," seems to the client to be grossly overstating the case.

Answering Personal Questions

Interviewers are frequently troubled by the personal questions clients ask them. Sometimes they are embarrassed and do not know what to answer or indeed whether to answer. If we can judge correctly the reasons back of such questions, the appropriate response will often be indicated.

A client may ask personal questions merely because he wants to be polite or thinks it is the social thing to do. He may not be interested in the answer, and in such cases if the discussion is directed back to his own problems he will be glad to continue with what is to him a much more absorbing subject, himself.

Often such a question as, "Do you play bridge?" "How old are you?" "Are you married?" may indicate simply the interviewee's natural curiosity about the person to whom he is in turn telling so much.

Again personal questions may indicate the beginning of the establishment of that closer relationship between the interviewer and interviewee discussed in Chapter Two. The interviewee is interested in finding out something about the personality and interests of the interviewer. He is testing him out, wanting to know what sort of person he is, in order to know whether his real personality corresponds to the one the interviewee is beginning to picture in his mind.

In most instances a frank, brief, truthful answer to a personal question is usually desirable. Normally this should be followed by an immediate redirection of the client's attention to himself. One danger is that the interviewer, through embarrassment, may become involved and tell too much, more than the client is really interested in knowing. This directs the client away from his own problems rather than toward them.

At other times an interviewer becomes involved in personal questions because he has failed to grasp their significance. Often such queries are not really personal but constitute rather the client's way of introducing a problem of his own which he would like to have discussed.

An older adolescent boy, absorbed with the problem of whether to marry or not may be trying to give the worker an indication of this concern and his desire to discuss it by a question, "Why aren't you married?" A brief impersonal answer leading on to a question about his own ideas about marriage will open the way for the client to pursue his own problems, which may involve such things as worry over leaving his mother or fear he can't support a wife.

Attractive young women interviewers occasionally find it difficult to maintain a professional relationship with a man, especially an adolescent boy or an older man. In their eagerness to be helpful they sometimes over-respond and, without realizing it, lead the interviewee to believe that they are personally interested in him. Then they are very much embarrassed when asked for a date. They have failed to make clear in their manner the professional nature of the relationship. Had they done so the interviewee, though attracted, would have gauged the interviewer's interest correctly as a friendly desire to help.

When such misinterpretation of the professional nature of the relationship does occur, instead of becoming frightened and withdrawn, the interviewer can best handle the situation by frankly telling the client that she feels she can be of most help if she sees him only during interviews and if they center their discussion primarily about his difficulties. At the same time she should scrutinize her own attitude to make certain that she has not fallen into certain mannerisms that would lead a client to expect too much from her.

Sometimes an interviewer deliberately introduces his own personal interests into the discussion. He may admire the interviewee's flowers or dog and add comments about his own likes and dislikes. Or to encourage the client to talk about his early experience he may tell the client that he too is from Texas and reminisce with him about the locality and people mutually known, or he may even enter into a discussion of politics, unions, or religion. Although at times such devices may be successful in helping the interviewee to feel acquainted and relaxed, the value of their use except in rare instances is dubious. Their dangers outweigh their possible value. With the introduction of the interviewer's personal opinions and feelings, the relationship may leave the professional level and become a social give and take or, worse, an argument. It is better for the interview to proceed with the client as the focus of attention, for his ideas and opinions rather than the interviewer's are paramount in the professional relationship.

Interviewers sometimes fall into the error of trying to win their clients' approval by praising the attractiveness of their clothes, the exquisiteness of an Italian woman's crochet, or the cleanliness of the kitchen. There is a distinction between an honest natural appreciation of such things and flattery or patronage. If the interviewer's interest is genuine, an expression of it may help in furthering the interview, but if it is a "technique" whose purpose is to flatter the client, this artificial intrusion will be sensed by the client. A saccharine effusiveness on the part of the interviewer is as offensive to a troubled person as irritability.

Leadership or Direction

From all that has been said thus far it may seem as if the interviewer assumes very little activity and direction, since so much stress has been put upon leaving the client free to express himself in his own way. Indeed, the inexperienced interviewer often feels as if the client were running away with the situation, setting the topics for discussion and determining the pace of the conversation, so that all the poor interviewer can do is try to keep track of what is being said. Actually, however, the skilled interviewer does assume leadership throughout. He consciously decides to allow the client to express himself. He knows the function and policy of his agency; he knows, in general, the areas in which he may be of service to the client; and with these things in mind, he guides the conversation along paths that enable him to determine whether or not he is going to be able to help the client, and if so, in what respects. He first directs his questions along the lines of allowing the interviewee to express his need in sufficient detail so that he may understand him better and know whether he will be able to help or whether he will need later to refer the case to someone else. He unobtrusively directs the interview throughout, deciding when to listen, when to talk, what to observe, and so on. With the over-talkative person who is inclined to ramble, or the old person whose mind tends to wander, he gently but sympathetically leads the interviewee back and redirects him through leading questions to a discussion of the immediate situation.

The difficulty in acquiring the appropriate degree of leadership in interviewing is well illustrated by the following report from a beginning student of case work.

At first I seemed to be off somewhere when opportunities presented themselves to guide the client in expressing his feeling at a given moment. I sat like a stick and when later asked by my supervisor why I hadn't done this or said that, I answered, "I don't know." Then I went to the opposite extreme. I progressed not only to the point where I learned to insert "Why?" but I carried questioning so far that often, as was pointed out to me later, I had switched what was on the client's mind to some other track. However, I am learning to listen again. It's a different sort of listening than I did when I sat petrified lest by speaking I stop the client's flow of conversation entirely. It is a more intelligent listening that is the outgrowth of the little bit more assurance I have. I am beginning to listen because I realize that this is what my client wants, rather than because I do not know what to say that may help him express himself. If I do ask a question or say something it is to show him I understand or want to help him say what he is finding it difficult to tell me and not, as previously, because I am shaky in my position and feel I have to say something so he'll know I am there and that I am the interviewer. You learn and learn and what remains to be learned seems to grow and grow.

The question of what material is relevant is not as simple as it might seem. Frequently material which seems irrelevant to the inexperienced has, because of the common tendency to disguise and distort and misplace one's feelings, considerable significance. It may be necessary to let the client "ramble on" for a while in order to clear the decks, as it were, so that he may get down to things that really are on his mind. On the other hand, with an already disturbed person it may be important for the interviewer to know when to discourage further elaboration of upsetting material. This is especially the case where the worker would be unable to do anything about it. An inexperienced interviewer might, for instance, be intrigued with the bizarre elaboration of material that the psychotic produces, but further elaboration of this might encourage the client in his instability. A too random discussion may indicate that the interviewee is not certain in what areas the interviewer is prepared to help him and he may be seeking some direction. Or again, satisfying though it may be for the interviewer to have the interviewee tell him intimate details, such revelations sometimes need to be checked or encouraged only in small doses. An interviewee who has "talked too much" often reveals subsequent anxiety. This is illustrated by the fact that frequently after a "confessional" interview the interviewee surprises the interviewer by being withdrawn, inarticulate, or hostile, or by breaking the next appointment.

In certain types of interviewing the interviewer is called upon to give advice and to offer suggestions, sometimes to formulate rather concrete plans of action and even to bring some influence to bear on the client to adopt a plan of procedure. It is always a problem how far direction of this sort should be carried.

The interviewer in a social agency is there primarily to serve the client. His problem is how best to make his help effective. Many of his clients come seeking advice. They feel that a person in the interviewer's position is equipped to give expert advice and they expect that when they ask for it, it will be proffered them. If the interviewer has sound advice to give and if his client is free enough of conflict to be able to accept it, it is probably wise to offer it. In many cases, however, advice is futile because the client is unable to act upon it. A woman in emotional conflict over her husband finds it difficult to accept advice either to divorce him or to remain with him. We can point out in such cases the probable consequences of the various alternatives that are available and stimulate the client to a course of reflection that may enable her to reach a decision for herself. For example, we can make clear the possibilities of getting a job, the legal procedures which would be necessary for a divorce, the steps to be taken in getting public aid, the possibilities of aiding her husband to make a better home adjustment, and so on.

Frequently people who ask advice really don't need it. Usually they have had plenty of that from relatives, neighbors, clergymen, or doctors. What they need is assistance in freeing themselves from some of the confusions in which they have become bogged down—additional information that will throw light on their situation, and encouragement to come to a decision of their own.

There are times when it is helpful to give a bit of advice to the client who demands it in order to test out his ability to use it, to challenge the mobilization of his energies so that both he and the interviewer may see more clearly whether he is able to profit from suggestions.

Again a bit of harmless advice may merely be a symbol to the client of our interest in him and willingness to try to help, whereas our rigid refusal to make suggestions may seem to the client an unwillingness to help.

Frequently the client who asks, "What do you think I should do?" —even the client who comes in with an eviction notice and seems to dump it helplessly in the interviewer's lap—when questioned as to whether he has any plans actually has several resourceful ideas.

If a worker who is asked for advice gives it because, perhaps, he fears that if he did not his prestige with the client would be threatened, he is really failing to utilize the client's own resourcefulness. In a surprising number of instances, the client who in turn is asked, "What do you think?" comes forward with ideas and plans of his own.

It is still more difficult to know when, if ever, an interviewer should go so far as to try to persuade a client to a course of action which he is reluctant to adopt but which seems to the worker clearly indicated. "A man convinced against his will is of the same opinion still." Many a persuasive interviewer has been disappointed by subsequent events. A foreign-born mother, afraid of hospitals, but "persuaded" to enter

45

her sick child, removes it at a critical period against the doctor's advice and then, if it dies, blames the interviewer. Yet it would be equally a mistake not to offer such a mother the opportunity of scientific care for the child. There is a distinction between persuading people against their will and generously offering them concrete help. One shouldn't simply neglect problems of health, budding delinquency, or the poverty of those too proud to ask for help. Of course, in certain agencies which have a primary responsibility to protect the community the situation is quite different and even forceful measures may be in order.

The case work interviewer should remember that his primary aim is to help his clients. If this desire is his basic driving one he need not be overly fearful that he will appear too inquisitive or too authoritative. There are occasions, especially in certain types of cases, when an interviewer represents some degree of authority to the client. If, however, his feelings are centered on the welfare of his client, this fact will break through the barrier of his authoritative position and be recognized by the client. If, on the other hand, the interviewer is absorbed in his own fears that the client will not like him and hence will not talk, or will regard him as nosey, then indeed the client will sense the interviewer's uncertainty and come to distrust his motives.

Where possible it is of course desirable not to appear to exercise authority but to lead the client to take for himself whatever steps are necessary. In general the things people do for themselves have more meaning for them.

If people find their own jobs, look for their own houses, make their own applications to hospitals, or other agencies, they are more likely to carry plans through. One person's way may not always be the same as another's, but each person has to work out his own manner of meeting situations. We must allow people a large measure of self-determination.

On the other hand, a worker should not allow his theory of self-determination to become actually a cloak behind which he withholds giving the client the help really needed. It is possible to give so little direction that the client profits not at all and is not even helped to know what help is available.

Interpretation

The interviewer's first aim, as we have said repeatedly, is to understand as fully as possible his client's problem. To do this successfully he must interpret the many clues to the underlying situation which the

46

client presents through his behavior and conversation. Rarely is the client sufficiently self-conscious to know and be able to give a straightforward account of the crucial factors that lie at the base of his difficulty. The interviewer must discover these for himself by going beneath the surface of his client's remarks and understanding their more than superficial significance. Just as a physician must look beyond the symptoms, say, fever or a bad cough, to the cause of his patient's illness, say, pneumonia or tuberculosis, so the case work interviewer must look for the underlying anxiety or fear which is symptomatically indicated by hostility or dependency or chronic invalidism.

Juvenile stealing, for example, may express merely a desire to be "one of the gang," or an unrealized need for revenge because of harsh home discipline, or, of course, any one of many other things. Failure in reading on the part of a boy with a high I.Q. may possibly be due to poor eyesight but is more likely to be a consequence of some emotional conflict such as ambivalence about growing up, fear of competition with a smarter younger sister, and so on.

The experienced interviewer will constantly be framing hypotheses as to the basic factors in the case confronting him, testing these, rejecting most of them, tentatively retaining others, seeking further confirmation and so on. In this process we must put 7 and 8 together to make 15, but we should take great care not to make 49 out of them. For example, when a woman in speaking of her husband "accidentally" refers to him as her father, the alert interviewer notes this but does not jump to the conclusion that her relationship to her husband is to an unusual degree that of daughter to father. He recognizes this as one possibility and keeps his attention open for corroborating evidence. In practice many of the tentative hypotheses one forms have to be discarded. Flexibility, the ability to change our hypothesis with the appearance of new evidence, is a trait well worth cultivating.

For an interviewer to interpret for himself is essential; for him to pass his interpretations on to the client is usually inadvisable. It is tempting to reveal our discoveries; for example, to say to a client, "Your blustering shows that you are really afraid." But if an interviewer is interested in helping the client, he will ordinarily keep such interpretations to himself. A client can profit from the interviewer's insight only if it becomes also the client's insight and this transfer cannot usually be made in so many words. The client must arrive at his own conclusions at his own pace. To be told that he feels anxiety, rejection, fear, and so on, will not help him. He must come to recognize

47

the existence of such feelings himself with sufficient conviction so that he can voluntarily acknowledge their presence.

Once an interviewer realizes the existence of such underlying factors he can often help his client to a recognition of them through discreet questions and comments, which include some element of interpretation. A client who is afraid to talk may be encouraged by a query such as, "You are not quite sure I understand?" or by an interpretative question such as, "You are afraid I will blame you as your mother has always done?" This last question would be appropriate only if the client had already been able to express fairly freely his feeling of rejection.

In general, by encouraging a client to elaborate more fully, the interviewer helps him see for himself the relationships between the various things he has said. A man may talk freely about his hatred for his father and again about his "so and so" boss. A worker will have helped him to understand, that is, to interpret, the situation, if he can be led, by further discussion, to a recognition of the connection between these two hatreds. Often interpretation consists in opening lines of communication between two previously isolated compartments of thought.

In a few cases where a secure relationship has been established between client and interviewer, we may wisely proffer a more direct interpretation. If a puny, precocious, "mother's boy" looking longingly at a group of boys playing baseball remarks, "I don't like baseball," we may perhaps say gently, "You really mean that you would like to be out playing with them, but that they don't like you?" We would do this, however, only if we were sure that the boy felt certain of the worker's affection. In such a case the worker's expression of this thought for him might well be a relief. It would indicate to him that the worker really understands him and that it is not necessary for him to make painful admissions. If the worker had made such a comment early in his relationship with the boy, it would have appeared only as an accusation to be resisted. A sense of proper timing is important for an interviewer. Often what cannot be said earlier should be said later. With regard to many questions or remarks, it is not a question of their goodness or badness but of their appropriateness at a given time.

Very often it is unnecessary ever to bring to a client's clear consciousness truths about himself of which the interviewer has become fully aware. It is important to remember that an interviewer's goal is sel-

48

dom if ever to achieve a complete personality change in the client. As a result of changes in little ways and of slight modifications of attitude, people often come to be able to make their own decisions and work out their most pressing problems without having become consciously aware of the many factors that the interviewer may see in the situation.

VI.

THINGS TO LOOK FOR IN INTERVIEWING

IT WILL BE HELPFUL for the reader to devise some method of studying interview records, his own or others. One helpful device is to check with various symbols the more important aspects of interviewing to which attention has been called. The interviews of Part Two furnish good material for such an enterprise.

For instance, with one symbol check every recorded instance of the worker's activity, including gestures as well as questions and comments. These may then be studied more readily to note the amount of worker activity and the kind. Were the comments made inserted to obtain further information, to encourage elaboration, to reassure, to indicate appreciation of the client's meaning, to restate and emphasize, or to refocus attention and redirect the course of the interview? Do they block or confuse the client or indicate understanding of him? Do they probe too deeply, proceed too fast, become argumentative or sarcastic, or are they sympathetic and appropriately timed?

So also, we may want to check and consider other aspects of interviewing. The following list is only suggestive. In addition to the items mentioned, we may want to examine an interview for certain specific matters such as mention of relief, alcoholism, job experiences, illness, and so on.

Association of Ideas

The phenomenon of free association is well known to the lay public. It has been publicized by William James under the name of "stream of consciousness" and by such fictional writers as James Joyce and Ernest Hemingway. It is worth while to be aware of its operation both in the client and in the interviewer. When the client mentions something such as lying, divorce, a grandmother, there may be started in the interviewer a stream of association which has little to do with the client's feelings about these things. The interviewer needs to recognize his own associations, as otherwise they may operate unconsciously. That is, he may read into the client's problem feelings that he has but that the client may not have. On the other hand, if he listens for the client's own free association, he will gain many helpful clues about the things he is discussing. A father may be telling about his son's running away and instead of continuing logically in this discussion of his son may begin telling about his own early runaway escapades, indicating that to him his son's behavior is not a separate episode but is entangled with his own feelings carried over from his childhood. A mother may be telling about her inability to get along with her husband and switch suddenly to talking about her parents' separation when she was a child and her unhappiness and shame about this, thus indicating that her own current problems are not isolated but are connected in her mind with her parents' similar difficulties.

Shifts in Conversation

It is frequently difficult to understand why a client suddenly changes the topic of conversation. The reason often becomes apparent through study of what he was previously saying and the topic he begins to discuss. The shift may be an indication that he was telling too much and desires not to reveal himself further. It may be that he was beginning to talk about material which was too painful for him to pursue, perhaps too personal or too damning. On the other hand, it may be that what seems to the outsider as a shift in conversation is really a continuation, that in the unconsciousness of the client both discussions have an intimate relationship. For instance, the interviewee may be discussing his difficulties with his foreman and suddenly begin discussing his childhood and the beatings his father gave him. The relationship in his own mind between his foreman and his father becomes obvious. Or he may be discussing his mother and suddenly make a personal remark about the woman interviewing him, indicating that in his own mind she in some way reminds him of his mother.

Opening and Closing Sentences

The first words a client says are often of unusual significance. Even though they are about the weather, they may indicate some reluctance to accept the professional nature of the interview and a desire to keep it on a polite, social level. Frequently the way in which a client first expresses his request gives the key to his problem and to his attitude about seeking help. He may start out with, "I don't suppose you can help me but . . ." or "I came because So-and-So sent me." The manner in which he first states his problem always bears special study.

Concluding remarks are also noteworthy. Often a client's last remark indicates either his summing-up of what the interview has meant to him or the degree to which his own forces have been mobilized for going ahead and working out his problem.

Recurrent References

In studying interviews we often notice a theme song. A client continually returns to a certain subject. This may be specific—a job, relief, his difficulties with his wife—or it may be more general. For example, we may detect throughout an interview repeated indications of difficulty with authority. The client complains about unjust treatment from his landlord, his father, his wife, and so on. Another person may reveal the theme of inability to express hostility. We may note that he is continually denying his own irritation. He starts to complain and then makes allowances.

Similar to repetition is the situation when the client "talks in circles." He talks freely enough, but does not move forward. He repeats the same ideas over and over. A man complaining about the unfairness of his budget repeats and repeats his complaints, unswerved by the worker's explanation of agency limitations. A mother tells over and over again the story of her childhood or of difficulties with her husband. Such circularity presents a stumbling block to any interviewer. When we have become aware that such an impasse has been reached, it is necessary to devise ways of inserting something new into the ritual, thus breaking up the circle and transforming it into a spiral. Here the interviewer's choice of a subject to insert is often guided by clues the client has given, perhaps some topic that has been mentioned before but not explained. If we have no clue, we may even have to make an insertion blindly, by trial and error. Questions such as, "What would you like to do about it?" or, "How would you like to have your husband act?" may stimulate the client to move into new and more profitable areas of discussion.

Inconsistencies and Gaps

We may note that the client's story is not unified. He often contradicts himself. His real meaning is not clear. Such behavior may indicate the operation of such internal pressure as guilt, confusion or ambivalence.

A man may report that he finished high school and later tell how he has had to work full time since the age of ten. Another may seem sincere in his statement that he is bending all efforts to find a job and yet be unable to mention specific places where he has applied.

Or again, a client may tell a straightforward story but with unexpected gaps, areas in which the interviewer finds it impossible to elicit information. Frequently these areas are of particular importance. A man may carefully neglect to give any reasons for leaving his last job. A woman may discuss in great detail certain difficulties she has been having with the children but say nothing about her husband. The significance of such gaps or inconsistencies often becomes clearer through their cumulative force. One such occurrence may suggest a barely possible interpretation. But if ten others confirm this hypothesis, it is no longer a mere possibility but a probability.

Concealed Meaning

It is essential for the interviewer to accustom himself to listening to what his client means as well as to what he says. The little boy who doesn't "like baseball" is clearly suffering from "sour grapes," since he is friendless and unable to get on with children of his own age. Usually, however, the presence of concealed meaning is not as obvious as in this instance, and often it is only with the most careful observation of slips of the tongue and attitudes and other clues that the interviewer can obtain any increased idea of the client's total meaning.

An unmarried mother who protests that she doesn't even want to see the father of her baby again may be concealing her infatuation for him and her hurt that he has "left her in the lurch."

Sometimes clients practically announce the presence of concealed factors. A woman may say, "I don't know whether it's a job I'm worried about or other things." In a first interview it might be wise to concentrate attention on the job, but at a later stage it would be well to inquire about the "other things."[1]

A fine example of concealed meaning is furnished by the following incident:

At an afternoon tea in New England, attended by members of both sexes, a woman made a remark to the effect that the English public school system tended to make men brutal. All in this group took sides, some agreeing and some disagreeing with the generalization. A heated and lengthy discussion followed in which the merits and demerits of the English public school system were thoroughly reviewed. In other words, the statement was taken at its face value and discussed at that level. No one, seemingly, paid attention to the fact that the woman who made the statement had married an Englishman who

---

[1] *Management and the Worker* (Roethlisberger and Dickson), Harvard University Press, 1939, p. 273.

had received an English public school education and that she was in the process of obtaining a divorce from him. Had it occurred to the others, as it did to one person in the room, that the woman had expressed more clearly her sentiments toward her husband than she had expressed anything equally clear about the English public school system, and that the form in which she expressed her sentiments had reacted on the national and international sentiments of her audience, which they, in turn, had more clearly expressed than anything equally clear about the English public school system, such an idea would have been secretly entertained and not publicly expressed, for that is the nature of polite social intercourse.

But in an interview things are otherwise. Had this statement been made in an interview, the interviewer would not have been misled by the manifest content of the statement. He would have been on the alert for a personal reference, and, once he had learned about the woman's husband, he would have guided the conversation on this topic rather than on the English public school system. Furthermore, he would have been on his guard not to allow any sentiments which he as a social being might entertain toward the English to intrude into the interview.

VII.

ESSENTIAL CONDITIONS OF GOOD INTERVIEWING

THERE are certain more concrete details in interviewing which should not be overlooked. Understanding and skill may be invalidated unless certain specific preparations are made for interviewing and certain precautions are taken. These may be listed under the general headings: (1) Physical Setting of the Interview, (2) Recording, (3) Confidential Nature of the Interview, and (4) Background Knowledge of the Interviewer.

Physical Setting

The physical setting of the interview may determine its entire potentiality. Some degree of privacy and a comfortable relaxed atmosphere are important. The interviewee is not encouraged to give much more than his name and address if the interviewer seems busy with other things, if people are rushing about, if there are distracting noises. He has a right to feel that, whether the interview lasts five minutes or an hour, he has, for that time, the undivided attention of the interviewer. Interruptions, telephone calls, and so on, should be reduced to a minimum. If the interviewee has waited in a crowded room, for what seems to him an interminably long period, he is naturally in no mood to sit down and discuss what is on his mind. Indeed, by that time the primary thing on his mind may be his irritation at being kept waiting, and he frequently feels it would be impolite to express this. If a wait or interruptions have been unavoidable, it is always helpful to give the client some recognition that these are disturbing and that we can naturally understand that they make it more difficult for him to proceed. At the same time if he protests that they have not troubled him, we can best accept his statements at their face value, as further insistence that they must have been disturbing may be interpreted by him as accusing, and he may conclude that we have been personally hurt by his irritation.

The length of the interview is, of course, so dependent upon the purpose of the interview that no optimum period of time can be fixed. In case work practice, however, it has been found that there is a great advantage in having the client know ahead of time that he will have a certain amount of time by appointment and that he may use it all or not as he wishes. In some types of agencies the interviews are as brief as fifteen minutes, in others longer periods are necessary. In general, it is seldom helpful to have the interview last more than an hour. Long interviews, lasting several hours, exhaust both client and worker. They may indicate that the client has been trapped into telling more than he wanted to, or that the interview has been inefficiently conducted so that too much time has been consumed in rambling. The fact that the client knows that his interview will terminate at a definite time may stimulate him to organize his material and present it concisely. Rather than have too long an interview it is probably wise for the client to have time to digest and think over what he has said and what has been said to him. After the lapse of an interval permitting this, a second interview will be more effective. It gives the client a greater sense of direction and security if he and the interviewer fix a definite time for the next appointment, rather than leaving it to him to "come in again some day."

It is desirable that an interviewer should have time between interviews or during the day to think over each interview quietly and note any significant aspects of it. Though efficiency is important, it cannot be measured by the number of interviews conducted within a given period. Efficiency in the interview relationship is proportional rather to the adequacy of understanding that is obtained, understanding that will make effective help possible. In the long run, the greatest efficiency will be achieved by giving the client during the interview comfortable surroundings, undivided attention, and ample time to express himself.

The discussion thus far has assumed that most interviews will take place in an office. There are, of course, many cases when interviews are of necessity or from choice conducted elsewhere, for example, in the home or at a person's place of employment or in a school.

The advantages of an office interview are obvious, since it provides greater opportunity for quiet and freedom from distracting interruptions. In addition it is frequently preferred because in general when people seek out help for themselves they are more likely to make use of it. The initiative required in leaving the home and going to an office is often an indication of the ability the client has to exercise some self-direction.

The fact that this is so frequently true is no indication, however, that we should make it a universal rule to refuse to visit clients. There are times when the client is unable to come to the office, and there are other times when he needs help and may later be able to bring himself to seek it actively. If the interviewer is rigid in his refusal to go out and offer his services, he may lose an opportunity to help where he is really needed. A person's failure to come into the office may have been due to his ignorance of the nature of case work service. In such a situation a "sample experience" of what the agency can offer may alleviate his natural distrust of the unknown.

Recording

If an interviewer can set aside a few minutes immediately after each interview for jotting down full notes concerning it, he will be saved the necessity of making many notes during the course of the interview itself. It is always something of a question how far note-taking during an interview is wise. There are usually certain factual things — names, addresses, dates, ages, places of previous residence or employment, and so on — which are normally written down as soon as they are mentioned. The interviewee regards it as perfectly natural for them to be noted and is not disturbed by the momentary pauses needed for writing them out.

If note-taking goes much beyond this, however, the interviewee may easily feel that he does not have the interviewer's full attention and may be distracted from the normal progress of his account. Similarly the interviewer's own participation may be interrupted or blocked by the exigencies of writing. Certainly when dynamic material is coming out the full attention of both interviewer and interviewee should be on this material itself. Even where an interviewer has an outline which must be filled in he does not need to do so slavishly in one, two, three order. Often the answers to many questions come out naturally in the course of the interview and can be inserted later.

A beginner may need to make a number of notes as he goes along. An open notebook where these may be jotted down unobtrusively is of great help. With practice he finds that he can rely increasingly on mental notes rather than on physical ones. Just a word or two in the already open notebook suffices to enable him to recall a whole phase of the conversation. With still more practice he finds that he can recall in amazing detail the full course of an interview.

The all too common carry-over of the college practice of filling notebooks with devitalized details must be given up and replaced by understanding listening combined with guiding participation. An interviewer's primary attention should be, not on the future record to be made of the interview, but on putting the client at his ease, encouraging him to talk freely, guiding his conversation into the desired paths, interpreting and reinterpreting the clues given by his words and behavior, in short, on understanding his situation and his need and on thinking about the most effective ways of helping him.

Confidentialness

When a person goes to a doctor or a lawyer, the confidential nature of the relationship is well established. The confidential nature of the interview relationship is often less well recognized. When it is established, beneficial results accrue at once. Frequently in interviews after some reassurance as to their confidential nature the interviewee is able to go ahead and talk freely about what is troubling him, even giving information which if generally known might involve him with the courts or create further family discord.

If interviewers are to build up respect for the confidential nature of their relationship with clients, they must in practice warrant this respect. As has been suggested, because of the relationship between the interviewer and interviewee, the interviewee is often lead to reveal himself more fully than he has to others, and it is the interviewer's responsibility not to misuse these confidences. It is sometimes tempting to tell incidents from an interview as anecdotes in a social gathering of colleagues or lay people. This may seem harmless because it does not directly affect the client, but actually it should be avoided as it gives the impression to others that we take the confidences given us lightly. Often, too, such careless talk suggests that our attitude toward our clients is a patronizing one.

Many agencies have strict rules against ever removing a record from an office, not only because of the danger of its loss but also because of its confidential nature. It goes without saying that a case record should be perused only in privacy. The subway is no place to read a case record even though one is too hard pressed to find time to read it in the office.

Background Knowledge

There is a certain body of knowledge, some specific and some general, which it is the responsibility of an interviewer to possess. The specific knowledge concerns the special purposes of the agency with which he is connected. An information clerk in a department store would need to know where to direct anyone who wishes an article sold in the store, but she would not be failing in her responsibility if she did not know the ferry schedule to Staten Island. An interviewer in a relief agency needs to know budget making, residence laws, and so on, but need not know the train schedules which a Travelers Aid worker would have on the tip of her tongue. A Red Cross worker needs to know many army regulations unneeded by a worker in a child-placing agency. The amount of such specific information required is often considerable, but it varies greatly from one agency to another. On the other hand, there is a more general body of knowledge every interviewer, no matter what agency he is associated with, should know. This would include, at a minimum, the topics discussed in this pamphlet.

PART TWO

SELECTED INTERVIEWS

THE discussion of the following interviews is presented not as exhaustive but as suggestive. It will be helpful if the reader, before proceeding to the discussion of each interview, will note in his own mind what he regards as the significant points of the interview in order to compare his views with the discussion that follows. If his own thinking does not follow the lines of this particular discussion, there is no reason to be surprised or concerned. There are many different ways in which these interviews might be discussed, and each individual will inevitably make his own selection of certain points for special emphasis.

The primary objective is to learn to analyze interview material and to think constructively about it rather than merely to absorb "the story" in a passively receptive way. Any method that promotes this active thinking about the interviewer's problems and interviewing techniques is helpful. One method, that of checking the material for a number of crucial factors, we have mentioned in Chapter Six.

If this were a pamphlet about case work, the discussions of the interviews would have to be carried much further. Those who are interested in case work will find it helpful to supplement their thinking about the interviewing methods by a consideration of the case work principles involved. Two of the illustrative interviews are from fiction and seven from the records of case work agencies. In the latter, all names and identifying information have been disguised.

VIII.

"Only A Conversation"

A N INTERVIEW from fiction is convincing in illustrating some of the points discussed, because in fiction the author is able to present the subjective feelings of the client, whereas in real interviews we have a report of only his objective behavior. The additional subjective material that the author gives us is frequently just that which the interviewer is seeking to obtain from the client.

The following interview illustrates many of the salient features of interviewing we have discussed.[1]

Today, as always on days when the cannery was closed, Mrs. Kazalski wavered between relief at having free time for housework and distress at the loss of a day's earnings. Good, at least, that the weather was fine, she thought; and told Katie to take her cough out into the sunshine, and to see that the baby did not cut himself on the oystershells. Then she sent Dan to the pump, at one end of the "camp," for water, and turned to sort an accumulation of soiled clothes, which smelt unpleasantly of stale oyster-juice.

Mrs. Kazalski accepted the distasteful odor with a dull fatalism, as she accepted the rest of her widow's lot; as she accepted everything in her life. A careless observer might have called her broad pleasant face stupid, might never have guessed that the thick crust of acceptance covered a shrinking sensitiveness, and had nothing to do with her thoughts. These, in so far as she thought at all, concerned themselves with obvious things: Worry over Katie's cough, the debt at the company store, a mingled hope and dread of the early call of the factory siren on the morrow; for an early siren meant a big load of oysters, and consequently more nickels.

She had put the clothes in to soak, when she become aware of excitement in the camp, and the sharp voice of Mrs. Oshinsky's Annie in breathless recital. Mrs. Kazalski put her head out of the door, and saw a group of women and children — Katie among them — at the end of the building.

One of the women called her, and in the next sentence told Mrs. Oshinsky's Annie not to talk so loud. She arrived in the midst of the hushed importance of Annie's outpouring.

"Gov'ment ladies. It's men dressed like ladies. Two. One went to talk to the boss. Mike Salinsky says it's inspectors. The other went down to the lower camp, but she says she ain't a inspector. She'll be here after a while. If they catch on us kids is working, you got to pay fines. Twenty-five dollars, Mike says. He says the gov-ment pays them to be inspectors, and that's why things cost so much at the store. He's awful mad. He says if it wasn't for

---

[1] Viola I. Paradise: "Only a Conversation." Reprinted by permission of author and publisher from *Atlantic Monthly*, January, 1923, p. 81-93.

inspectors, everything would be better for us. He says maybe they'll take the work away from us. He says maybe they'll put us in jail. I think maybe they got revolvers!"

After some discussion, Mrs. Kazalski spoke. "It ain't nothing. They can't take money we ain't got. If we keep our mouths shut, they won't know the children work. The cannery ain't running today. Everybody's got to tell their children to shut up, and to shut up themselves, only be polite. No gov'ment lady or man neither won't get something out of me."

All morning as she worked, however, she worried about the gov'ment lady. Suppose that someone should let it out. Jail? No, surely not that. But if they should stop the children from working, how could they live? Suppose the company should refuse credit at the store. Once she had wished to cheat the Virgin Mary of a half-burned candle. Could this be punishment?

And suddenly, athwart her numb acceptance of life, came a passionate regret; if only she had never left Baltimore. Why, why, had she yielded to the persuasions of Mike Salinsky. She went over in her mind all the incidents that had influenced her to "come South to oysters." The day of Mike Salinsky's visit stood out as clearly in her mind as if it had been yesterday, instead of the day of her husband's funeral, three months ago.

[The story continues with Mrs. Kazalski's introspection as she goes over in her mind all that had happened between the time of the funeral, three months ago, and today. She thinks of how she sat after the funeral, dazed, wishing only to be alone, but being pestered by her sister-in-law with, "What are you going to do now?" At last the sister-in-law left and then suddenly there appeared the smooth, oily, but persuasive Mike Salinsky with the offer, "How would you like to go South? How'd you like to go to the Gulf of Mexico, down in Mississippi where it's nice and warm, and where you and all the children could get nice easy work, and good pay, and free rent, and free fuel? How'd you like to go South and shuck oysters and pick shrimps for the winter? I'm row-boss for the O. U. Oyster Company, and they sent me up here to get families to come down and work." It was particularly the lure of the warm South and his assurance that Katie's cough would get better there that finally persuaded her. She recalled all the awful disappointments upon her arrival. The miserable one-room accommodations in a long, sagging twelve-room row, the back-breaking work, the change in Mike to a brutal boss, prodding her and the tiniest child through the long working hours, the high prices at the company store and the ever-increasing debt piling up there, and above all the worry over Katie's increased coughing. Now, added to this was the agonizing fear that the government ladies would find out about the children's working.]

Mrs. Kazalski struggled hard against despair. If only she had never left Baltimore!

And now the government, the government was sending inspectors, to fine them, to starve them, to take the work away from their children! Twenty-five dollars! Suppose they discovered that her children worked, that she had not the twenty-five dollars? Some of the neighbors might let it out. Well, the government lady would get nothing from her, not a thing. She would be civil, but not a word about the work!

The government lady was in the door. "It's not a man, dressed as a woman," was Mrs. Kazalski's first thought. "Annie Oshinsky is a fool!" She responded, unsmiling, to the "Good afternoon, Mrs. Kazalski. I'm Miss Egmont of the Children's Bureau. May I come in?"

"Sit down," she said, in a dull voice. But she thought, as she looked at the short, slight, brown-clad figure, the pointed piquant face under the close-fitting little round hat, "She looks — almost — as if she could be happy!" It came as a revelation to her that any adult could look like this.

Afterward, thinking of her, Mrs. Kazalski wondered why she had seemed so remarkable. She was not pretty, nor yet clever; apparently she had not noticed Mrs. Kazalski's hostility, had acted as if she were welcome. She had said, easily, "May I take off my hat? It fits a little too tight"; and, without waiting for permission, had removed it and hung it on a knob of the chair.

Afterward, as during the interview, Mrs. Kazalski felt about in her sparsely furnished mind for a word to explain this visitor, so unlike anyone she had ever met. The Polish word for "separate" kept coming to her mind; but, being unused to abstract thinking, she did not recognize it as exactly the word to express Miss Egmont's detachment — detachment for herself, apparent freedom from problems of her own — which was a quality that puzzled and attracted Mrs. Kazalski.

Mrs. Kazalski's reflections about the worker reveal that the interviewee as well as the interviewer is observing, sizing up, speculating. We note Mrs. Kazalski's recognition that the interviewer has not responded to her hostility or retaliated in kind. The interviewer's first activity indicates an easy relaxation. She asks, "May I come in?" "May I take off my hat?" but proceeds unhesitatingly to do both without waiting for an answer. Mrs. Kazalski's rather incoherent thought of the interviewer as somehow "separate" shows that she recognizes her questioner is not using this occasion for personal gratification but is primarily interested in her. This mutual interplay constitutes the beginning of the establishment of the interviewer-interviewee relationship. Miss Egmont is sensed by Mrs. Kazalski as being a person free of all problems. Actually she undoubtedly has, as does everyone, worries of her own, but Mrs. Kazalski senses that she does not let them intrude into the interview.

This interview has a certain special interest in view of the fact that the government lady represents authority and must begin the interview by forcing herself upon the client. It illustrates how she overcomes this initial handicap and later developments show that in spite of it she was able to be of real help to Mrs. Kazalski.

"Did you ever hear of the Children's Bureau?" began Miss Egmont. And when Mrs. Kazalski had said, "No'm," she continued, "Well, it's a part of the government that is trying to find out how children and mothers are getting along, and what they do, in order to learn what things are best for them.

"Now we are visiting all mothers with children in these little canning camps. How many children have you?"

Mrs. Kazalski was immediately on her guard. Miss Egmont's pencil was poised over a large card, on which Mrs. Kazalski could see irregular patches of printing, combined with blank spaces, and red-and-blue lines. Miss Egmont was not looking at the card, but at her hostess, with half-smiling encouragement. And surely, thought Mrs. Kazalski, that was a harmless question. No harm, either, in giving their ages and telling at what grades they had stopped in school. In fact, Miss Egmont turned directly to Katie and Dan, who stood by, their wide eyes upon her, and asked them questions about school. Katie, who coughed most of the time, coughed harder now, from nervousness; and Miss Egmont's face clouded, as she asked about the cough.

Since Miss Egmont has sought out Mrs. Kazalski, she begins the interview with a brief explanation of the purpose of her visit. Notice here that she does not confuse the client by a long and involved explanation which would at this point be meaningless. Later, as we shall see, when it has more meaning, Miss Egmont gives a fuller explanation. Here her simple straightforward account not only serves to give Mrs. Kazalski an intellectual understanding of the reason for her visit, but also, by its informality and friendly tone, serves to reassure Mrs. Kazalski and to indicate that the interview will be not a third degree but a mutual discussion of a common problem.

The client's sensitiveness to minute details is illustrated by her noting that Miss Egmont, though asking questions from a card, was looking at her rather than the card. (A client once told her family case worker that she would not go back to the relief agency because the worker there "did not even look at me but just wrote down the answers I made to her questions.") The sense of receiving the full attention of the interviewer encourages conversation and accelerates the progress of the interview.

Miss Egmont "begins where the client is" — that is, she begins with simple innocuous questions which stimulate the client to talk and do not frighten or threaten her by seeming to plunge too quickly into "dangerous" areas. Mrs. Kazalski is naturally unready to talk freely until she has had an opportunity to acquire more confidence in the stranger. In every interview there are simple "identifying information" questions which can be used as a springboard from which to progress into more important matters. They serve as an opportunity for the interviewer and interviewee to get acquainted and test each other.

Despite her resolution to be circumspect in her dealings with this intruder, Mrs. Kazalski scarcely listened to what she was saying, so preoccupied was she in her personality. "If she had my life and my troubles," she thought, "would she be so — so different?"

"You 'Merican lady?" she asked.

"Yes," said Miss Egmont. "But my grandparents came from the old country. How long have you been in America?" "Nine years. How old are you lady?" If Miss Egmont was surprised, she did not show it. "Thirty-two," she replied. "And you?"

Mrs. Kazalski's eyes opened wide. Thirty-two! Why, she herself was only thirty. She would have guessed Miss Egmont fully ten years younger. Then surely this apparent happiness was not real. Why, she was not married; was an old maid.

Mrs. Kazalski softened, with something like pity. So busy was she speculating about her visitor, that she answerd questions mechanically. But suddenly, one question brought her up short.

"Now tell me about the children's work. I suppose Katie can't help you very much at the factory, because of her cough?"

Mrs. Kazalski's face hardened. She made no answer. Miss Egmont might ask till doomsday, she'd get nothing out of her. Yet it was strange that she should ask the question so directly — not at all as if she were trying to surprise an answer from her.

Mrs. Kazalski inserts a personal question, "You 'Merican lady?" This is an expression of her natural curiosity and of the beginning of the relationship being established between them. Miss Egmont answers matter-of-factly and contributes an addition that her grandparents came from the old country, in order to give Mrs. Kazalski a feeling that she does not feel superior because she is American and that she, too, though more remotely, has a "foreign" background. She uses this opportunity, though it may not have been the next question on the card, to ask how long Mrs. Kazalski has been in America.

Then Mrs. Kazalski's speculations are broken into with a question which is more dangerous to her, "Now tell me about the children's work." She is shocked into silence, but already some confidence has been established, and her interest has been aroused. Mrs. Kazalski recognizes by the open, direct way in which the interviewer asks her question that she is not frightened, insecure, or defensive.

"I'd like to know," Miss Egmont went on, in her soft, even voice, "about the work you and the children do in the cannery—just what you do, and how much you earn, and what time you go to work, and some other things. But first, are you sure you understand just why I'm asking these questions? Sometimes people are suspicious, can't understand why the government, far off in Washington, should send someone away down here to ask questions. Maybe you'd like to ask me some questions before you answer mine?"

"Mrs. Oshinsky says you come to collect the fines."

"Fines?"

"The twenty-five dollars for people, if their children work. You inspector?" "No," said Miss Egmont, simply, and it surprised Mrs. Kazalski that the accusation did not embarrass her. "There are inspectors," Miss Egmont continued, "and there are fines for employing children; but the bosses, not the workers, pay the fines. Only my work has nothing to do with fines. The government is making a study of what's good for children and what's bad for children. You see, children are the most valuable things in the world; but it is only lately that people have learned in order to make them healthier and happier, we have to study them, and see how things affect them. The Children's Bureau is finding out how work affects them—how it affects their health and their chances of growing up strong and healthy, and happy. What do you think about it? How do you feel about the work your children do, and the other children?"

Mrs. Kazalski had never thought of it. But the question turned her scrutiny back from her visitor to herself. It half flashed through her mind that she had never before thought of anything aside from how to get money for the next day's living; how to keep her children and her house clean; what to cook; whether the oysters would be large or small; how to pick out the wettest car and to work quickly, so that as much water as possible would get in with the oyster-meat, before it was weighed.

But now, here was a new thing. Her opinion was being asked. She shrugged her shoulders. What had she to do with these things?

Here Miss Egmont gives a little further explanation and straightforwardly anticipates for Mrs. Kazalski some of the questions which will later be asked. She has sensed Mrs. Kazalski's "hardened face and unwillingness to continue." She expresses her recognition of this by asking: "Are you sure just why I am asking these questions? Maybe you'd like to ask me some questions before you answer mine." This again gives Mrs. Kazalski the feeling that she is sharing in the conversation, that Miss Egmont wants to understand her and is not merely routinely pumping her. The wording of this question is more encouraging than, say, a blunt query such as, "Have you any questions?" which might merely discourage elucidation. Through this question Miss Egmont discovers the worry back of the hardness, the fear that the worker is there to collect $25. Without this question or a similar one encouraging the client to express herself, the worker might have attempted to conduct the interview without having any clues as to why she met with such stubborn resistance. Now she knows "what is on the other one's mind" and can deal with that fear rather than struggle with the stubbornness which was the external manifestation of it.

In the explanation that she gives of the work of the Children's Bureau, instead of assuming dogmatically that it is right and that Mrs. Kazalski should answer questions she again elicits Mrs. Kazalski's participation by asking her, "What do you think about it?" Mrs. Kazalski is startled and encouraged by having her opinion asked.

Yet something quite strange and new seemed to be pushing up in her mind. A slow anger was part of it, but there was another element in it, too. She had an opinion, and she wanted, not to be silent and sullen with this government lady, but to talk, to argue with her. Presently she was answering: "I think too bad for children to work; but what you can do? It's better to work and live, than to starve and die. What would poor people without husband do, if the children don't work? Without the children, I no could make half to live on. Even with the children, I got a debt eighteen dollars, at the store. And you—the government—it don't give money, no? No, just questions it gives. How can help us—questions? The row-boss say you get money for questions, that's why things cost too much—for tax. You say it's good for children—questions. Will it help my children?"

This was a long speech for Mrs. Kazalski. She was breathing hard and perspiring with the effort of it.

Miss Egmont's face was thoughtful. "I'm not absolutely sure it will help your children." She spoke slowly, experienced in making simple people understand new things. "I'm not sure the results of a study like this will come soon enough, though they may come in time to help the younger ones. Do you know," she went on, "that some states give money to widows, so that their children can go to school? And that, in some countries, fathers and bosses and the government together pay for insurance, so that, if the father dies, the mother will have some money every month, and won't have to put the children to work? Well, how do you suppose those countries and those states came to do these things? They sent people like me to go and study what the people needed, how they lived and how they worked; and they then planned ways to help them. But it takes time, and to learn these things we must depend on what the workers tell us, and what the bosses tell us. You, when you tell me about your children's work and about your work, are helping the government to make things better for all children, even though the changes may not come tomorrow or for several years. I believe they will come in your children's lifetime. Don't you want to help make things better for children?"

Mrs. Kazalski felt strangely moved. Only partly by the argument of her visitor, only partly by the visitor's personality. Mainly, it was the fact of this visit, the fact of this conversation, which had swerved her mind from its familiar groove into the rough vastness of new thinking. To think, for the first time in one's life, of anything outside the range of one's experience and observation, is a profound experience. As Mrs. Kazalski's untutored but not stupid mind followed Miss Egmont's simple explanation, she forgot about her debt to the store, forgot Katie's cough (for Katie, listening intently had not coughed for some minutes). A strange emotion welled up in her, a feeling of value, a feeling that her children were really important, not only to herself, but to the country.

The elicitation of Mrs. Kazalski's opinion enabled her to release some of her pent up hostility just as the previous straightforward question as to whether Mrs. Kazalski understood why Miss Egmont was there had released the fear back of her sullenness. The expression of hostility also furthers the progress of the interview, because with its expression Mrs. Kazalski feels some lessening of the tension she had been exerting in repressing her hostility. Furthermore, her account gave Miss Egmont considerable new understanding of the situation.

Mrs. Kazalski's challenge, "Will it help my children?" does not, as it might have, put the interviewer on the defensive. Consequently she is not tempted to reassure Mrs. Kazalski falsely. Instead she takes Mrs. Kazalski's question seriously and tries to answer it honestly without making glowing promises. Frequently an interviewer, when challenged as to whether or not he can really help, is impelled by his own uncertainty to offer dogmatic assurances which serve as much to reassure him as the client.

Since Mrs. Kazalski has shown by her willingness to express herself that she now has some confidence in Miss Egmont, the latter feels able to offer a more detailed explanation of her work. She does so basing her account on what she has learned thus far about the client. Using familiar language she lets Mrs. Kazalski know that she is a part of the study and that she can help by talking frankly. Miss Egmont talks about things which Mrs. Kazalski can understand, children, school, jobs, rather than about abstractions such as child labor, democracy, and so on. "Don't you want to help make things better for children?" appeals directly to Mrs. Kazalski's own interests. Children are something which she knows about. She lives with them and for them every day.

Mrs. Kazalski is moved "only partly by the argument . . . only partly by the visitor's personality." This reflects the difference between intellectual and emotional understanding. She understands the meaning of Miss Egmont's words but she also senses the feeling behind them, the desire to help. A sense of personal dignity stirs in her a feeling that her ideas are important and that what she can say will be really helpful.

She shook her head several times. "It should be a good work," she said slowly, at last. And when Miss Egmont took up her questioning again, with, "How did you happen to leave Baltimore, to come down here?" Mrs. Kazalski found herself wanting to tell the whole story of her hardships. It would be blessed relief to talk about her troubles, to put them into words, to a person quite detached from her life, someone she would never see again. Never had she done this; never had it occurred to her. She had always thought of her burdens as inevitable, inflicted by Providence, goading her to laborious, irksome effort, which offered no reward. She was not a woman to pity herself, but now, as she poured forth her tale, it was as if she had been given the power to stand apart and see herself; and a rush of self-pity, the first she had known, flooded her for the moment—a strange indulgence of pain that was hotter, but softer, than the hard accepting silence of her many months. Yet there was nothing in her voice, no moisture in her eyes, to tell Miss Egmont, who listened with understanding, of her emotion. She had sent the children out of doors, and in a low voice—that her neighbors might not hear—she had begun:

"Things were enough good with us, till the accident. After five months sick, my man dies; and was left in the house only five dollars thirty-eight cents. Katie coughed bad. That night the row-boss—"

She told of Mike Salinsky's visit, of her trip down, of her disappointment; of the draughty coldness of the canning shed in bad wet weather; how the roof of her house "leaked like a basket" when it rained; how she lay awake at night, too tired to sleep, worrying, waiting for the siren, yet dreading it; waiting and dreading the watchman's pounding on the door, which never failed to fill her with anger; hating to force the children from their beds at four or five or six o'clock in the morning—according to the size of the catch; how fast the shucking gloves wore out—"one glove a day, and we cut our hands yet"; how much worse picking shrimps was than shucking oysters, because of the acid in the head of the shrimp; "after two days at shrimps, my hands look like butchershop, but that's the only one thing to make think there is in the world meat! And the stink! You smelt it once? So!!"

But, worst of all, was the worry about Katie's cough. That kept recurring again and again in her outpouring. She talked with the simple vividness of a person unused to fluent speech. "I no would care about work, I no would care for nothing, if Katie could get well. When I go away from Baltimore, I say, charity the Kazalski's no take. But now I think foolish to be more proud than to care of your child's health. It ain't proud, having them work over mud and wet, in clothes soaked and torn like noodles. And I think maybe oysters no good for the cough."

Mrs. Kazalski is now able to tell her story freely, and as she talks a new idea begins to evolve; "Through talking" it takes on more definite form. "Now I think foolish to be more proud than to care for your child's health."

"Did you ask the boss if he would send you back now, instead of waiting till the end?"

Mrs. Kazalski laughed bitterly. "He gave me a mouthful," she said.

"Excuse me, I tell you all this," she went on, "but you want to know why children got to work. That's why. But if Katie could get well, I'd give—I'd give—well, I ain't got nothing to give. Excuse me, miss, your face looks very sorry. But you ask—and now you know."

Miss Egmont was silent for a while. Then she said, "Did your husband's boss do nothing for you when he died?" "Why should he do something? It was no his fault—the accident. My man, my man—" she paused, "—he good worker, nine year one boss; but he make himself the accident. Sixteen hours he work, and he was much tired. He was a good worker, but we no could ask something from the boss, when my husband make the accident." "When you get back to Baltimore, what will you do?"

Mrs. Kazalski had asked herself this same question many times, and never had she found any answer. But now, miraculously, she discovered that she had a plan, a plan that sprang up of its own accord, that rushed forth, almost as a part of her outpouring.

"I go to a charity. I say, 'Let me take money for rooms; I take lodgers, so I can get a doctor for Katie; I take in washing; I pay back the money.' Maybe I pay neighbor to take care of baby; I go to factory, maybe. But I send my children on the school; they should grow up, like you say, like people, not like pigs. What for I leave Baltimore, to come down to this pig-life, I don't know. If only," she added wistfully, "if only Katie should live till we get back."

Miss Egmont looked away, out of the open doorway, to the Gulf. The water was a deep blue. A white sail moved slowly, in the sunlight, along the horizon.

"Well," she said, bringing her eyes back to Mrs. Kazalski, "you have had a hard time. But there are only six weeks more, and you say, you have been here nearly fourteen already. Six weeks is not so terribly long. About the debt, I should not worry too much. Are you the only person here with a debt at the store?" "Oh, no! All people got debt at the store!"

"Well, surely the company won't want to keep all of you here, for your debt. At the worst, they will take some of your bedding to pay for it. And there may be a heavy run of oysters. And thank you very much for giving me this information. Would you mind if I look over this card, to see that I haven't forgotten to ask anything? I'm supposed to have an answer for every question."

Mrs. Kazalski did not accuse her of indifference. Her mind was so occupied with her sudden, new plans for the ordering of her life on her return to Baltimore that she was scarcely conscious of Miss Egmont.

Miss Egmont stayed a few minutes longer to get in detail the earnings of each member of the family since their coming, and the hours of work. Presently she left, hoping things would go better, hoping Katie would improve, suggesting a Baltimore clinic.

Mrs. Kazalski's recital concerns recent events, and we may assume that this is one reason why she was able to obtain so much release from airing her troubles. If her present predicament had been due to more remote causes, this outpouring would have been less effective.

Miss Egmont's question, "Did you ask the boss if he would send you back now?" is a question which implies a plan yet is quite different from, "Why don't you ask the boss if he will send you back?" as it

71

suggests a possible procedure without in any way forcing it upon the client. It also leaves the client entirely free to make her own plans.

The interviewer's next question about workmen's compensation is for information. Then, "When you get back to Baltimore, what will you do?" is a question to stimulate Mrs. Kazalski into making a plan for herself. It is practical and realistic, in contrast to the emotional recital of Mrs. Kazalski's recent experiences. It serves to channel Mrs. Kazalski's aroused feeling into practical plan-making. In answer to this question Mrs. Kazalski "miraculously" discovers that she has a plan.

Some may be inclined to feel that this is fiction, that in real life it couldn't have happened this way. But experience indicates that such "miracles" are not uncommon. The interviewer was wise in letting the plan come from Mrs. Kazalski. Had she proposed one to her it would not have been accepted with the conviction and emotional support of one that was self-originated.

Then with some reassurance about the debt, Miss Egmont winds up the interview on a more practical note, returning to the details of filling in her card. Just as it is unwise to plunge quickly into an interview, so it is always wise, if the content of an interview has been rather emotional, to take some time before leaving to discuss rather more matter-of-fact details so as not to leave the client at the height of an emotional state.

Mrs. Kazalski went back to her washtub. She could hear Miss Egmont making the same explanation in the next compartment, could hear her neighbor's guarded, reluctant answers. She did not listen to the words, though she could easily have heard them—at first. But after awhile her neighbor had some trouble as real as her own; perhaps—why, surely every woman in the camp had troubles. Most of them were widows, most of them had children to support. And perhaps other women, all over the country! Why, of course, it was right that the government should send someone down to see how things were!

That night she went to bed with a new feeling. It was as if, for the first time in her life, she was fully alive. Not happy, but awake. Sometimes, in her youth —say, fourteen years ago—at a wedding in Galicia, after a pleasant dance, she had a feeling akin to this, yet different. Then the dancing made one forget the hard furrows and the heavy plow. Now there was no forgetting, rather a full remembering, a coming alive of her mind. A full remembering of herself, and, therefore, of others.

Yet, she told herself, nothing had happened, really. A woman had come, had asked questions, had gone away. She had answered questions, had stated her situation. "Yet nothing has happened," she repeated to herself in Polish, "only a conversation. Talk, only." The debt was still unpaid, Katie was this minute coughing, and life in Baltimore, at the end of six weeks, would be a hard struggle, even though she now had a plan. . . . Why, then, this new courage, this strange, warm feeling, which reached out, even beyond this roomful of her own family—which included even more than the whole camp? Was this, she asked herself, what they meant by patriotism?

The wind blew, and the single palm tree outside her door cracked. The sound was like the rattle of hard rain. Other nights she had hated it, had thought it mournful, but now she liked it. She raised her head from the bed, and through the window she could see the tree. The moonlight seemed to drop off the sharp fingers of the leaves. Splotches of light and black shadows made a grotesquery; and for the first time she saw a beauty in it. She could close her ears to the heavy breathing of her neighbors, and to Katie's cough, and could listen to the orchestra of crickets and frogs, against the night's outer silence, with—was it possible?—almost with happiness.

Perhaps the outstanding quality of this interview is the skill revealed in getting a reluctant person to talk. The change from, "No gov'ment lady nor man neither won't get something out of me," to the free outpourings of Mrs. Kazalski's story is remarkable.

One might well question the wisdom of letting Mrs. Kazalski tell so much when this was known to be a single contact and when the worker was not in a position to do anything about Mrs. Kazalski's grievances. She has to gather up her cards, fill in a few more blank spaces, and move on to the next of several hundred women in the camp. One is justified in speculating about the extent to which a worker under such circumstances should let the interview proceed. Many of the women in the camp undoubtedly have similar difficulties, and we may well question whether "only a conversation" will be equally effective in every case. Is there not perhaps more likelihood in such a procedure of stirring up rather than resolving anxieties?

An important consideration is the fact that although the interview stirs up a good deal of feeling it is feeling centered largely around recent and current experiences. Actually the worker does not go into Mrs. Kazalski's past or attempt to get at deeper motivations. Another safeguard in this interview is the very fact that both interviewer and interviewee knew in advance that this was to be a single contact. Mrs. Kazalski was not led to believe that she would continue to see the worker and get further help from her. The worker's limited purpose in talking with her was stated clearly throughout, thus tying the interview to a known firm basis.

It should not be concluded that the sort of "catharsis" provided here by "Only a Conversation" would always be so effective. If Mrs.

Kazalski's present dilemma were only one link in a long chain of disastrous experiences, she would probably have got no release from thus unburdening herself.

The interview does show, however, that when the circumstances are favorable, a skilled interviewer can render invaluable service in the course of the interview itself.

IX.

"I Can't Go Through It Alone"

THE following interview from a medical social service department illustrates a worker's skill in discovering and alleviating anxiety hidden beneath a belligerent exterior.

The case worker was alone in the office when Mrs. Stewart appeared in the doorway and looked questioningly around. In response to worker's greeting she inquired whether this was the Social Service Department and when given an affirmative answer she walked in and seated herself. She was a rather nice-looking brunette young woman, twenty years old. She seemed ill at ease as she lighted a cigarette and began to smoke vigorously. The worker asked if there was any way in which she could be of help to her. Mrs. Stewart promptly replied: "Yes, I want to get a statement from the doctor that I'm sick and can't work." Before the worker had an opportunity to reply, Mrs. Stewart continued. "I guess you wonder what is the matter with me because I don't look sick. That's the trouble—I'm too darned healthy. Why couldn't it be me instead of some of those other women down there in that clinic that's got a bad heart or something else. I sit down there and think how easy it would be for them to get a statement and they don't need it. But I do, I really do."

As she finished talking she looked at the worker, laughed rather nervously, took her hat off and tossed it on the desk. The worker said: "Suppose you tell me why you need a statement so much." Mrs. Stewart replied rather aggressively: "Well, I'm not going to tell you all my life history because you don't need to know it. The fact is that I'm about three months pregnant, and I can't go on working in the factory any more. It makes my back hurt and my heart go fast. I'm not welcome at home since I've stopped working and I'm not bringing home money, so I'm staying with my married sister temporarily. But I can't go on staying there because her husband hasn't much of a job and she's got a lot of kids. I want that statement so my family will believe I'm sick and let me stay at home without nagging me all the time."

At this point, Mrs. Stewart ran her hand through her long bobbed hair and then leaned forward with her face in the palm of her hand, thus creating quite a picture of despair. The worker inquired whether Mrs. Stewart had spoken to the doctor in the clinic about her desire for a statement. Quite petulantly she replied: "Yes, I told him I wanted it. He said he could give me one saying that I was pregnant but he wasn't willing to say I was too sick to work. He seemed to think it would be good for me to work for the next six months. Said a lot of pregnant women work up until the last month." Impulsively she leaned over and took hold of the worker's hand. "Can't you see that's not the kind of a statement I want? It wouldn't do the trick. I have to have one that says that I'm sick—awful sick." The worker said: "I can see that you are pretty desperate all right and that you must be in quite a predicament or you would not want to

75

be sick so badly." At this moment there was an unexpected outburst of tears. Between sobs she managed to say: "I'm in a fix all right. My husband's in the Army and I want to get him out. Oh! I'll just die if we have to be separated." The worker commented: "No wonder you want him out so badly. It is hard to face your first pregnancy alone."

Mrs. Stewart continued to sob as she said that they had been married in a hurry so he wouldn't be drafted and then he had to go because the draft board discovered that their marriage took place after his number was called. She described, a little hysterically, how he had run away without leave one night in order that they might be together and that his commanding officer had let him off easy because he said he could understand how things were. "I guess it was then I got in this shape. We didn't mean to, of course, but we love each other so much and somehow we didn't think about the chances we were taking." The worker inquired quietly: "And now that you are pregnant, how do you feel about having a child?" Mrs. Stewart stopped crying abruptly and said: "Oh, gee! I want him a lot. A lot of my girl friends are married and have babies. We'd been married sooner only both of us wanted to work and save our money so we could have a kid."

Her enthusiasm waned again and she tearfully added: "But I can't go through this alone. He'll desert from the Army or I'll do something to make myself awful sick so he'll have to come home." The worker said: "I doubt if it will be necessary for you to do either." She then explained the procedure of filing a formal request for discharge with the commanding officer, who in turn would refer the request to the American Red Cross for investigation, who would get in touch with the hospital about a confirmation of pregnancy. After this explanation, Mrs. Stewart was thoughtful for a few seconds and then she asked quietly: "And suppose—suppose that doesn't work?" Worker replied: "It will be hard but I think you can do it." There was quite a long silence before the patient said: "I see what you mean. You think I can go through with it alone." The worker nodded and then added: "Yes, there are women who have to do just that." Quite unexpectedly Mrs. Stewart leaned over confidentially and said: "Well, I guess men aren't allowed in the delivery room anyway, are they?" She was assured on this point and they laughed together about the suffering which expectant fathers undergo, during their lonely vigil in hospital waiting-rooms. Mrs. Stewart was still smiling as she got up abruptly, put on her hat, and said: "Well, I'll tell Jim to speak to his C.O. but if that doesn't work, I guess it's 'chin up' for me."

A little later, the worker met Mrs. Stewart as she was coming from the obstetrical clinic. She greeted Mrs. Stewart by inquiring, "Is it still 'chin up'?" To this Mrs. Stewart replied that she had told the doctor she never felt better and that she was glad she was good and strong and really could go on working if she had to.

Here, as throughout every interview, the worker is confronted by a multitude of possible responses among which to choose. Many of these flash through her mind almost without her being aware of them. Without time for deliberation she selects that one which at the moment seems to her best. Fortunately, it is often the case that any one of a number of possible choices would have been equally reasonable. On the other hand, of course, there are many responses she could have made which, instead of helping, would have blocked, discouraged, inhibited, or frightened her client. The ability to choose the most effective response quickly and surely comes only with practice and training. One helpful way of improving this capacity in ourselves is to study interviews in retrospect — our own and others — and try to imagine and consider the many responses other than the actual one which might have been made.

In this interview we note again the worker's discerning observation. She is immediately aware of signs of tension and disturbance in this otherwise self-sufficient, healthy appearing young woman of twenty: vigorous smoking, taking off her hat and tossing it on the desk, and generally aggressive responses. Under the sympathetic recognition of desperation by the worker she breaks down and cries.

The worker's first response is her question as to whether there is any way in which she may be of help. Consider, for instance, what might have been the result if in this case the worker had felt it necessary before proceeding to obtain full application material and had insistently asked the client to give information. Or suppose she had felt the need of first explaining to the client the function of the social service department. In either case she would have lost the spontaneous response of the client and probably would have diverted her from expressing her real concern. Instead the worker offers help in a general way and allows the client to follow her own train of thought.

Mrs. Stewart's first statement about wishing she were as sick as the other women at the clinic might well have stimulated the worker to some such thought as, "How silly to want to be sick," or "How unreasonable," or, "You ought to be grateful that you are healthy." Instead she recognizes that although healthy the woman is disturbed and her comment, "Suppose you tell me why you need the statement so much," indicates that she can comprehend the possibility that a well person might want to be ill. The client's aggressive reply, "Well, I'm not going to tell you my life history!" indicates to the worker that the client, though asking for help, wants to keep the reins in her own hands and maintain some independence. It indicates also, that although asking for help, she resents the need to do so, and that she has a feeling that in asking for help she may be putting herself under obligation to the worker and may be giving up some of her own independence. The worker evidently assumed that Mrs. Stewart does have some "personal history" which she is concerned about.

The worker may have had in her own mind two possibilities, one that Mrs. Stewart really did not want to reveal her personal history, and the other, that her belligerent denial indicated she really wanted an opportunity to tell more. In the light of these alternatives the worker let the matter drop for the time being but later gave Mrs. Stewart a chance to talk more freely.

A perhaps natural but certainly unwise reaction would have been for the worker to respond to Mrs. Stewart's aggressiveness with aggression or argument. She might have thought, at least to herself, "You don't need to have a chip on your shoulder. Who said I was going to probe and force you to tell more than you want to?" Or she might have felt, "How do you expect me to help you if you are so resistive and unwilling to have confidence in me?" Instead, the worker again notes the client's real despair and asks realistically, as if she had accepted the client's need to be sick as natural and reasonable, if Mrs. Stewart has asked the doctor in the clinic for a statement that she can't work. This question is for information and also gives the client reassurance that the worker understands her need for the statement as real.

The worker's understanding of the situation is summed up in her comment, "I can see that you are pretty desperate all right, and that you must be in quite a predicament or you would not want to be sick so badly." This positive comment indicates greater acceptance on the part of the worker than would, for instance, the question, "Why do you need to be sick so badly?" The latter might have seemed accusing to the client since she had just implied that she did not want to be asked questions. The worker's comment constitutes an interpretation since it restates, in more significant form, material which the client has already given. Its accuracy is confirmed by the client's ability to reveal how upset she is. Again the worker's comment, "No wonder you want him out so badly. It is hard to face your first pregnancy alone," reveals to the client the worker's understanding and acceptance that the client's feelings do not seem unreasonable to the worker even though they may seem so to others. With this much reassurance she is able to let down the barriers of her defensiveness and tell a great deal about her feelings concerning marriage and pregnancy.

The worker's question, as to how Mrs. Stewart feels about having a child, served both to obtain information and, in case the situation

78

was further complicated by fear or by resentment of pregnancy, to give the client an opportunity to express her feelings. Mrs. Stewart's response clears this issue for the worker, who evidently feels convinced from the woman's spontaneous responses that she does want the child.

The woman's threat that her husband will desert or she will make herself desperately ill is responded to realistically with information which the worker has. The worker might well have been thinking to herself, "What a foolish woman," or have been tempted to argue or threaten her with the dire consequences of such a course. Her mere statement, "I doubt that it will be necessary for you to do either," implies no blame for having considered these alternatives and suggests that the worker realizes that the client is so desperate that either of these courses might seem necessary to her.

By this time the client has, even in this short contact, developed enough confidence in the worker so that she believes that the worker really wants to help her, is interested in her, and does not feel that she is foolish or unreasonable. Hence she can now accept what she would have been unable to earlier in the interview, that is, the worker's expression of confidence in her that she really can go through the pregnancy alone.

The shift of Mrs. Stewart's attitude from the beginning to the end of the interview is remarkable. We can see that the change is not merely fortuitous but took place directly as a result of the worker's handling of the situation and her self-conscious recognition of the forces that were at work in Mrs. Stewart. Instrumental also was the relationship built up between the two, even though the relationship was established in such a brief span of time. We can understand what happened when we contrast Mrs. Stewart, unhappy and misunderstood at home, left alone by her husband and rebuffed by her family, with Mrs. Stewart listened to understandingly and helped sympathetically by the worker.

Again we see how much need there is on the part of a human being to share his feelings with someone else and to know that there is someone who understands.

X.

"Nobody Wants You When You're Old"

THE following interview from a private family agency illustrates the interviewer's sensitivity in recognizing the confusions of an elderly woman and helping her in simple concrete ways to proceed in applying for W.P.A. work.

Mrs. Andrews appeared in Central Office with a letter from Mr. White, a lawyer. The letter was addressed to our agency and stated that Mrs. Andrews was destitute and had no one to assist her. She had $12 a month rent from a three-room shack she owned at Star Beach, but had got in debt recently because she was unable to find work. She was willing to work on W.P.A., or do anything, and Mr. White understood that a new W.P.A. project was to be started. "If you can help her in any way to get located or give her any suggestions as to what to do, I will deeply appreciate it."

Mrs. Andrews waited all morning to be seen. She was a tall, slender, gray-haired woman, adequately and neatly dressed. She was fully sixty years of age. When we were seated in the interview room I asked in what way she and Mr. White had thought we could help. She replied that there was to be a W.P.A. lunch project at the Lincoln High School and she would like to be assigned there. It would be difficult for her to take work anywhere else, because of transportation. She was living at Star Beach and could ride to the school on the school bus. I explained that our agency had no connection with the W.P.A., but said that we should be glad to give her information or help in any way we could. I said that applications for W.P.A. were made at the W.P.A. office and that the public agency was the relief agency. She said she would rather have work than relief.

In reply to my question, she informed me that her husband was dead, but she was divorced from him before his death and she did not know where or when he died. Until seven years ago she had worked for different people as cook and housekeeper. Nine years ago an old man for whom she had been keeping house died and left her "a few dollars." She built a little house at Star Beach, lived there and raised chickens, and did cleaning for people in clubhouses along the river. She was not successful with her chickens because feed was so high, and she had to get rid of them. Before building her house she had lived for a while with the Blacks at Star Beach. Then she rented her house and went back to board with the Blacks. She was to pay them $4 a week for her room and board, but had not been able to pay that much and was now in debt to them. Mr. Black was out of work and incapacitated. She felt it was unfair for her to stay there with them when she could not pay her board. She was receiving $12 a month rent and was paying taxes on the place out of this. Her tax bill this year amounted to $20.55.

I explained that I had been asking these questions in order to ascertain whether there was a possibility of her being eligible for W.P.A. I told her where application could be made for W.P.A. and mentioned a number of documents that she should take with her when she went there. At this, Mrs. Andrews moved impatiently in her chair and made a gesture with her hands as if she were pushing away the information I was giving her. She said there was no use, she could never do all that. She seemed to be feeling a good deal of discouragement and frustration.

I asked if she felt that it would be difficult for her to get work references now. She said yes, and everything was so muddled up. During the early part of the interview she frequently stuttered, her chin moving in a sort of spasm when she began to talk. After a while, however, she stopped doing this. I said perhaps she would like to talk about this feeling she had of being muddled. She replied that she didn't know how to tell me about it. I said I thought she probably felt pretty discouraged. She said yes, she didn't know what she could do. She ought not to go on staying with the Blacks. She was willing to do any kind of work, but people didn't want an old person to work for them.

I asked about her health. She said she was well, but had not a great deal of strength any more. I asked if she meant that she got tired, and she said yes. There would be no use, she said, in her trying to work on W.P.A. anywhere but at the high school. She knew they wanted people there and thought she might get on. I asked if she would work in the capacity of cook, and she said she would. I inquired about her experience. She said that until she had had her house built and gone to live at Star Beach she had made her living by working for rich people. She did cooking and housework. She had only the one child, a daughter who lived in the city, was divorced from her husband, and had a thirteen-year-old child. Mrs. Andrews did not speak of the daughter until I asked if she had children. She added that the daughter did not want to do anything for her and they seldom saw each other.

I suggested that I call the W.P.A. certification office for information as to what data would be required in Mrs. Andrews' specific situation, taking into account the fact that she had not been working recently except to do cleaning at the clubhouses. I thought at first that she was not interested in having me do this, and we talked some more about her situation. I came back to the matter later, asking directly if she wished me to make the call. She quickly said yes, she would be thrilled to have me do anything I could.

I telephoned the certification office and talked to Mr. U., who said there was no reason why Mrs. Andrews should not make application for W.P.A. She should bring her last tax bill, a statement from her tenant telling how long he had lived in her house, the amount of rent he was paying per month, and whether he was related to Mrs. Andrews. She should bring her bank book if she had ever had a bank account (he thought her legacy probably had been deposited in a bank), and should bring reference letters from people for whom she had worked, saying how long they had known her and what work she had done. These, I understood, could be from the people for whom she had cleaned in recent years. She should bring a letter from the Blacks telling of her financial situation, how long she had lived with them, and the amount of board she had paid them. If she had borrowed any money, she should bring letters from people who had made the loans. If she had any debts, she should bring bills or other information about them. If she had her divorce papers she should bring them, and should try to have in mind the place and date of her husband's death. Mr. U. said his office might need more information than this, but probably Mrs. Andrews could send it by mail after her interview there.

I made a memo for Mrs. Andrews of the information she was to take to the W.P.A. office. I commented that it sounded like a lot, but that it actually was very simple. She no doubt already had all these data. She said she had not her divorce papers and didn't know when or where her husband died. She seemed a little upset over this, and I said she could explain that to the interviewer at W.P.A. Nothing can be quite cut and dried. She said she had her bank book and her last tax bill. She appeared less panicky and thought she could get letters from people for whom she had worked, without any difficulty; also statements from her tenant and the Blacks.

She said she would have to go home to get these things. I said I should not advise her going to the W.P.A. office in the afternoon, anyway. It would be best to go as early as possible in the morning. She said it was difficult for her to get around, because of the amount of bus fare from where she lived. But friends had driven her to our office today, and she seemed confident of being able to find transportation to the W.P.A. office. I told her that when she made application no promise could be made as to where she would be assigned. She would receive the assignment later by mail. If she should be assigned to a project at a distance and one which she felt she could not reach, she need not be too upset. People were sometimes transferred to projects nearer their homes. Mrs. Andrews could ask the W.P.A. office for a transfer, or if she wished, we could do so. There would also be the question of whether, with W.P.A. wages, she would not be able to make trips to a project in another part of the county. She accepted this quite calmly and agreed that she might be able to accept an assignment at some distance. She understood there was no certainty of her getting the job, but we agreed that it would be worth while making the application.

I asked Mrs. Andrews if she thought she would like to talk with me again. She said she didn't know what she would talk about. I said she had spoken of being upset and I thought she might feel it would help to talk things over, particularly if she should not be assigned to W.P.A. In that case, she might want help in making some other plan. She readily agreed to this, and I gave her the address of the district office near her home, explaining that I would be there on Fridays. I had open office hours in the morning and could see people in the afternoon by appointment. As she left, Mrs. Andrews thanked me for the help I had given her and said, "Until I see you again."

The worker's first question is a general one, stimulating Mrs. Andrews to state the sort of help which she expects to get from the agency. Her response centers the problem and enables the worker to explain her own limitations in being able to help. At the same time she assures Mrs. Andrews that although she cannot actually obtain a W.P.A. assignment for her, she can be of help in gathering information about applying.

When the worker mentions the number of documents which Mrs. Andrews will need to take with her in applying to the W.P.A., she notes, "Mrs. Andrews moved impatiently with her hands as if she were pushing away the information."

The worker, having recognized how bewildering the requirements seem, does not respond with Pollyanna-like futile reassurance, such as, "Oh, I'm sure you can do it." Instead she first attempts to get a little more understanding of why these requirements seem so confusing. The comment, "I said perhaps she would like to talk about this feeling she had of being muddled," is a leading question, but so general that Mrs. Andrews does not know how to respond. She feels so muddled she doesn't know where to begin. The more specific comment, "I said I thought she probably felt pretty discouraged," proves more helpful. Mrs. Andrews is then able to go on and tell a little more about how she feels that "people don't want an old person to work for them." Further background information is then elicited about her experience. The definite offer on the part of the worker to call the W.P.A. certification office to ascertain the specific data which Mrs. Andrews would be required to submit indicates that the worker is willing to take over some of Mrs. Andrews' responsibility. The worker recognizes that Mrs. Andrews, because of her age and discouragement, is unable to take full initiative for her own application and needs to have the procedures made easier for her.

Particularly with elderly people, it is sometimes difficult to know how much responsibility they should be relieved of. They resent the implication of younger people that they are unable to manage their own lives. Although they seem at times bewildered and helpless, they really want to keep their independence. They want friendliness and interest, someone to listen patiently, but they want any important decisions left to them. They do not wish there to be any implication that they are not able to "carry on."

The worker is careful not to force her offer of help upon Mrs. Andrews. She merely suggests it as a possibility in order to see whether Mrs. Andrews really wants to take advantage of it. The worker did not yet know her well enough to be certain that what she really wanted was a job.

The worker recognizes that the list of requirements "sounds like a lot," but she reduces them to a written list which Mrs. Andrews may take with her, and makes them appear achievable step by step. The worker shows that she appreciates that the procedures seem difficult to Mrs. Andrews and reassures her as to the probability of her being able to qualify even if she cannot produce every detail requested. That her attitude is helpful is indicated by the remark, "Mrs. Andrews appeared less panicky."

Specific advice is given about the best time to apply and about the possibility of her asking for a transfer, and she is prepared for the possibility that she may not be able to get into the project which she wants. Knowing the various possibilities, she now seems more calm and able to "face the reality" that there is no certainty of her getting a job.

In the end the worker gives Mrs. Andrews an opportunity to come in again. Her first suggestion of this is so general that Mrs. Andrews responds that "she didn't know what she would talk about." The worker was then more specific in saying that she had spoken of being upset and "she might feel it would be of help to talk things over." The worker specified a regular time at which she could be found at the district office, but she left the decision to make use of this opportunity to Mrs. Andrews.

The interview seems to have helped Mrs. Andrews to see more clearly just what is involved. She leaves with specific next steps in mind rather than feeling vaguely muddled as she had been when she came in.

XI.

"Make Them Turn Their Lights Out"

THE following interview illustrates skill in shifting an individual's interest from a job he is unfitted for to one more suited to his personality and abilities. The interview was conducted in an Office for Civilian Defense by a case worker loaned by the local family case work agency.

Mr. Robertson came into the interviewing room with a rapid, precise stride. He brought with him his application form which he had filled out. As he handed it to me, he remarked that some of the questions were not worded very clearly, and so he felt somewhat handicapped in setting down his information. He lit a cigarette and leaned back comfortably in his chair while I scanned his application. I noticed that he was sixty years of age, although he looked no more than fifty. Under employment history I noticed that he changed jobs frequently. Among the different types he held were those of clerk, accountant, and floor walker. While I was looking at the application his eyes were sharply scrutinizing the room, taking in every detail.

Mr. Robertson had stated his first job preference to be that of air raid warden and had specified no second or third choices. I began the interview, therefore, by asking him why he wished to have this particular type of position. His answer was serious and intent. He realized the seriousness of these air raids and how important it was for all the citizens to co-operate or "toe the line" as he put it. He said he would like to see to it that there would be a hundred per cent co-operation in the district assigned to him. He had been talking to some of his neighbors recently about what the government might be asking them to do to help with general war plans and the neighbors had not taken the matter very seriously. Some had even said that they would like to see "anybody make them turn their lights out." This had irritated him considerably and he had apparently given them a lecture on good citizenship.

At this point he leaned across the desk confidentially and said he wouldn't be surprised if a couple of families in his neighborhood were fifth columnists. "They are always making remarks about the government and sometimes I wonder how far they should be trusted." He wondered if I thought he should turn in their names to us so that we could "report them." I explained that this was not a part of our job and that if he felt he had any real complaints about his neighbors he might go down and talk with one of the men at the F.B.I. This did not satisfy him entirely and he began to relate the details of some of their activities of which he was suspicious. I said that I could appreciate how concerned he was over these situations, but there were other people waiting to be seen and I thought it would be better if he would tell his story to someone who could take some action regarding it. Reluctantly he agreed to do this.

I then asked him how much he understood about an air raid warden's job. He proceeded to list the various responsibilities which indicated that he had read pretty carefully the descriptive pamphlet which was given to him with the application form. I was interested in the fact that each of these responsibilities he stated in a punitive manner, "Make the people turn their lights out, keep the people off the street, make the people go to the shelter," and so on.

Then he added with a gleam in his eye, "You know most Americans need a strong arm to get them to do things." I asked him what he would do if he came across a man who refused to obey orders. Without a moment's hesitation he responded that if the man were his size he thought he would "sock him" and get some other men to take him away, and if the man were bigger than he, he would call the police.

I asked him what qualifications he thought he had for this position and he replied that he was in good health, he was not "a drinking man" and he was "always on time," never late for work in his life. I commented that these were important qualifications and I was wondering if they might not be more useful in some other line of work than the one he had chosen. I said the government was anxious to know about each person's special abilities and skills so that the person might be placed in the particular job in which these qualifications might be used to greatest advantage. Mr. Robertson eagerly asked if I thought there was a better kind of job for him and then I suggested that he specify his second and third choices on the basis of what his work experience had best trained him to do.

Mr. Robertson then told me about his clerical experience and it developed that he was apparently exceptionally precise and accurate with figures. I encouraged to him to talk more about his work experiences and it developed that he seemed to get along at jobs quite well for several months and then he would become bored with the monotony and also critical of authority. In each instance the criticism seemed to develop to the point of his feeling justified in quitting and so that is the course he would take.

I stressed the advantages of this office training and pointed out that there would be far fewer persons with his qualifications than those necessary for air raid warden. I then asked him, "If the government would ask you to take a job which involved your skill with figures, would you accept it?" Magnanimously he agreed to do this, but then asked quickly, "Would I wear a uniform for that kind of work?"

I asked him why he inquired. Rather sheepishly he protested that he didn't know. He had just seen some pictures of the London air raid wardens and he guessed he was impressed by them. I said I guessed this was pretty natural after all and I wasn't sure whether or not he would be given a uniform, but he could be sure that whatever job he would be given it would be on the basis that the government felt it needed him in that particular spot.

He said that certainly was enough for him, thanked me and left.

The outstanding skill illustrated in this interview is the worker's ability to guide this man's planning into more constructive channels without in any way threatening him, punishing him for his punishing attitudes, or pointing out to him his unfitness for the air raid warden job. She refrains from any attempt to change his personality but rather redirects his energies into channels where he might be able to use them usefully instead of harmfully. Through her skilled questioning she first encourages him to reveal to her his unfitness for the job (but she doesn't tell him everything she knows). Then she proceeds by further questioning to discover what abilities he does have and to assure him that they are needed fully as much as are the services of the air raid warden. Thus he is able to shift his plans without any loss of his personal dignity, and at the same time the neighborhood is saved from what otherwise promised to be some unfortunate brawls.

At the end, one of his probable subjective reasons for wanting to be an air raid warden is revealed in his question about the uniform. We here get a glimpse, beneath the surface of a self-assured arrogant man, of a little boy impressed with his Indian or Boy Scout suit.

This interview presents a slightly different situation from any of the others, since the client is not seeking help in the sense of going to a social agency. There are many interviews in which this situation arises. The case worker does not have the responsibility of helping the individual with his problems but rather in determining his potentiality for meeting certain requirements. Typical interviews that come to mind in this connection are those with prospective foster parents or adoptive parents. They come to the agency not to seek help for themselves but to offer their services. It is the responsibility of the interviewer, however, to determine enough about their personalities and capacities to evaluate their ability to do the job for which they are volunteering. In these instances, the interviewer's primary responsibility is to protect his client, but in doing so he often has an opportunity indirectly to be helpful to the person who has applied.

XII.

"We Want to Go Home"

THE following interview from a Travelers Aid Society with a family in search of a defense job is illustrative of skilled interviewing meeting an emergency effectively and at the same time initiating steps that may help to improve the situation out of which the emergency arose.

Mr. Jones, his wife, and Sally, four years old, approached the Travelers Aid desk in the station. The day was cold and Mr. Jones did not have a top coat. Mrs. Jones was wearing a spring coat and no hat; Sally was dressed in a wine-colored snow suit. The black suitcase they carried was tied together with a string. They lined up before the desk, with Sally in the middle and each parent holding her hand. They all looked scared to death.

Mr. Jones began the conversation by saying, "We want to go home." I said, "Where is your home?" Mr. Jones said they lived in a small town in Pennsylvania. A minister had brought them to this town, let them off near the bus terminal, and suggested they come to the Travelers Aid Society. They needed $5.56 to get home, but they did not have the money. He added, "The last bus for Alton today leaves in an hour. Can you help me?" I said, yes, we could help him, but we would need more information, and at this point suggested that we go to the private office where we could talk more freely. I had addressed this remark to Mr. Jones, and he said, "We'll all go — we have stuck together so far." I mentioned that we were going to the private office because there were many people in the station, it was confusing, and we were constantly interrupted. It would be easier to talk privately.

After we arrived in the office, Mr. Jones sat near the desk and again assumed responsibility for the conversation. Mrs. Jones and Sally sat almost behind the worker. Sally was sleepy and said several times that she wanted to go home. Mrs. Jones took her in her arms and said she hoped they would be able to go home soon. I then picked up the conversation where we left off, summarized it by saying, "Before we came into this office you told me that you were eager to leave this evening for home, that you needed $5.56 for the fare to Alton, and asked whether we could help, and I had said that we could." I told them the way we could help them was to give them money for their bus fare, if we could verify that they belonged in Alton. Mr. Jones immediately reached in his pocket and pulled out a worn wallet saying, "I can prove that all right." The first card he presented was his Social Security card, giving his name and number; the next was his W.P.A. card showing he had received his last assignment in Alton in November, 1941. He mentioned the W.P.A. officers knew him well. Then he showed me his driver's license and car registration.

Mr. Jones continued that he had a house in Alton rent-free and when he got back he would get a food order from the relief until he went back to work on W.P.A. He guessed he would be glad to get it. I asked him why he would be glad to get it. He said that he had been to Rhode Island concerning defense work. His brother-in-law lives in Providence, and since he did not have much money and the brother-in-law lived in a defense industrial community, he thought that it was sensible to live with his brother-in-law while he looked for a defense job. He was there two weeks and found he could secure no work because he was fifty years old and they did not take men over forty, and because he could not read and write. He explained that he had worked all of his life without knowing how to read and write, but still he could not get a defense job.

They had enough money to return to Alton in their car and were on their way home in New York State when the main bearing burned out. At the garage where they had it repaired the mechanic told them he could repair it for $6. They spent the last $6 they had to have it fixed, thinking they could continue home without food. When they started the car something else happened to it and they had to leave it there. Mr. Jones then showed us the name of the garage where the car was. He had asked the garage keeper to sell it for junk and send him the money. It was a 1928 car and he doubted that he would ever hear from it. They hitch-hiked to a nearby city, spent the night at the Salvation Army, where they were treated very well. They started to hitch-hike home this morning when the minister picked them up and brought them as far as here. Mr. Jones said he would have continued hitch-hiking but the wind came up and it was so cold Mary and Sally could not stand it.

I asked if he had made up his mind that W.P.A. was the only thing he could get to do now. He said he was disappointed that he did not get defense work because they have lived on relief and a low income for so long and owed so many bills that they thought now would be a good time to pay up some bills and get some things they would like to have. He had heard younger men talking and they were all leaving Alton to get good jobs at $40 and $50 a week. I suggested that he continue a regular contact with his employment office; no doubt men his age would be needed in defense work later. I suggested that Pittsburgh, an industrial community near Alton, might have need of workers. Perhaps he could get something there later. He said he would never have enough money to take another trip. He had saved a long time for this one and now he would not have a car and it was expensive to travel otherwise. I said he might have friends who had cars who would let him use them, if it was a car that he needed. He doubted it, but I noticed that he was thinking about this suggestion.

At this point I heard Sally whisper to her mother, "Mommy, I am hungry," to which her mother replied that she knew she was, but she would have to wait. I suggested that Mr. Jones tell me when they had last eaten. He said that they had breakfast at the Salvation Army this morning and the minister had bought each of them a cup of coffee, and that was all they had had. I said, "Don't you need food for this evening and tomorrow morning until you can get to the relief department?" He said that it would be asking too much. If he could just get home, and then he added, "Of course, it is hard on Sally to go without something to eat." I said that we could advance him a dollar for food in addition to the money for the bus tickets for himself and wife.

At this point he mentioned that this was his first experience like this, and he had lived fifty years. He hoped it would be his last. He said it wasn't any fun being out on the road wondering what was going to happen next.

Sally was a pretty blonde child and I asked Mr. Jones whether he had other children. He spoke of a daughter who was very bright who was killed in an automobile accident a year ago. He said James, twelve years old, was in the sixth grade and was staying with his grandparents while they took this trip. He did not want his son to miss a day of school. He wanted him to get as much education as he could take. He did not want him to face the same problems that he had had to meet.

I said that Mr. Jones had convinced us that he belonged in Alton and we could give him the transportation and a dollar for food. He signed the receipt for the money and thanked us.

The worker immediately notes that the family look "scared to death" and at once gives them some assurance that she can be of help. Her sensitivity to their feelings is indicated by her taking them into a private office where they can talk more easily, and by here again allaying their obvious anxiety as quickly as possible with some assurance of help without waiting for full details. Her readiness to promise aid is a result of her diagnostic skill in quickly sizing up the situation. In another situation with, say, an adolescent runaway boy, the interviewer would not so quickly offer financial help unless she were certain that in doing so she would not run the risk of encouraging him to repeat such irresponsible behavior. Here, however, she quickly senses that being caught away from home without funds is not characteristic of this family. She realizes that the occurrence is so foreign to them that they are frightened by it, and she immediately reassures them and makes their return as easy as possible.

She helps them in stating their situation by repeating for them in the private office what they had told her in the busy station waiting-room, thus indicating to them her understanding of their problem and her willingness to take some share of responsibility in the interview. She obtains enough information to understand the nature of their immediate need and to guide her in deciding whether or not they should be referred to an agency in her home town upon their return.

Her questions serve also to assure the family of her interest in them, of her feeling that "they matter," and of her desire to help. They had been extremely disheartened. Their one effort to become again self-supporting had failed ignominiously and they were about ready to relax for good on W.P.A. assistance. The worker by her comments gave them new hope that other employment possibilities might arise closer to home in the near future and stimulated them to lay plans for taking advantage of such an opportunity.

XIII.

"What's Going to Happen to Me Now?"

THE following interview from a child placing agency shows how interviewing may be used in preparing a child for placement. By means of her friendly interest and considerate explanations, the worker is able to change the child's hopeless anxiety in the face of a new and frightening situation into an acceptance of the change and even a certain expectancy that it will mean better days ahead. The child is freed from the feeling of being "pushed around" by having her own energies enlisted in preparations for the change so that she feels that she is really participating in making it.

[Elaine, aged eleven, was referred to the intake division of a child placement agency by the children's court for placement away from home. The court report stated that for about a year Elaine's stepfather had been engaged in sexual activities with her. Elaine, who had been born out of wedlock, had already gone through a series of unhealthy experiences because of her mother's promiscuity.

The court had given Elaine physical, psychological, and psychiatric examinations and had found her healthy, intelligent, and friendly, but very much upset about her experiences with her stepfather. She had been afraid to confide in her mother because her stepfather had threatened to kill her if she did. The psychiatrist recommended that Elaine be placed away from home, at least until her mother proved able to maintain a stable home.

In considering the type of care that would best meet Elaine's needs, the agency decided that a cottage plan institution might be preferable at this point to a foster home. It was felt that it might be easier for Elaine to adjust first in an institution where she would have an opportunity to relate herself to children and would have a wider choice in selecting an adult with whom she could identify. In planning Elaine's first placement in an institution, the agency hoped that after she had had an opportunity to readjust her first concepts of an adult world, she might then be placed in a foster home.

At the time of the court's referral to the agency, she had already spent three months at a children's detention home while the court's investigation was being made. Her mother had opposed placement but was finally forced to accept the authority of the court. Because of the delay in referral, the worker had but two days in which to prepare Elaine for placement. The following are her accounts of her two interviews with Elaine.]

I first visited Elaine at the Children's Detention Home. Before seeing the child I arranged to take Elaine out for an hour the following afternoon. I saw Elaine for about 45 minutes. She was totally unprepared for my visit. She was completely bewildered by her present experience and had no idea of what was going to happen to her. She appeared quite terrified when she was brought down and introduced to me. Elaine is a small, dark, little girl, thin and pathetic,

91

with straight brown hair and a heartshaped face. She had tried rather unsuccessfully to improve her appearance by putting a little barrette into her hair. The faded and ill-fitting clothes of the home did not improve her appearance. Her eyes, which are very large and dark, were teary and several times tears welled up in her eyes and flowed down her cheeks. At times she seemed unable to speak because she would cry. In the midst of her tears she attempted to smile. Her lips would quiver. She would try to control herself, be unable to, would cry, then look up from under her lashes and try to brave a smile.

I introduced myself to Elaine telling her that the court had asked our help in planning for her. I said I knew that Elaine was pretty unhappy in the Detention Home and quite bewildered about what was going to happen to her. In so far as I could, in the short time that we had, I would like to help her. Elaine's face lit up and she tried very hard to smile, to show her appreciation, but it was difficult for her to smile without tears. Elaine and I spent some time discussing her present experience in the Detention Home. (Elaine had been there for three months before I saw her.) She told me that she had lost a good deal of weight since she had been there, both because she was unhappy and because she could not eat the food they served. She continued to talk about the Detention Home, expressing a great deal of resentment.

With a sad expression she said that she had been there longer than most of the children and she thought it was a very long time. The monotony was relieved a little by the fact that she had relatives coming to visit her. On the morning of the day I was there her mother, her sister, and her aunt had come to see her. With real feeling the child said, "My mother wants to take me home." She cried in a heartbreaking fashion. I said I was sure that her mother wanted to take her home; that perhaps it was not possible for her to go home yet. Her mother would first make a real home for her and then she would go to live with her mother. Elaine continued to cry and to say that she wanted to go home with her mother now; that she did not want to go anywhere else. With a sigh, the child said that she knew she really could not go home now. The judge had talked to her and told her that she could not go home until her mother had made a real home for her. In front of the judge her mother said that she would try to make a real home for Elaine. Elaine said she had accepted the fact that she would not be able to go home now. She was sure her mother would do everything to make it possible to take her home in the very near future. However, until that time she knew that some other plan had to be made for her. She did not know what that plan was. She felt sure that I could tell her.

Did it mean that I could get her out of the Detention Home? I said that that was what I wanted to do and that was why I had come to see her, to talk to her about what was going to happen to her. Elaine said that strange things had been happening to her. She didn't even know about courts and judges and "horrible places" like the Detention Home. I said that these were unusual experiences for a child and painful ones. Elaine cried bitterly and said the Detention Home was "like a jail" (the windows have bars) ; that she was so anxious to get out of it. She felt just as though she had a jail sentence, an indefinite one, since she had no idea when she would be getting out. She

92

hasn't even been out of the building for the past three months. I said I had made arrangements to take her out for a walk the following day. We would spend an hour together and Elaine could plan the hour in whatever way she liked. At this point Elaine gave me a really genuine smile and I commented on it, saying that I hadn't been sure she knew how to smile; that when she smiled her face lit up, she was so pretty. Elaine managed a laugh at that and said that she would spend the rest of her waking hours planning for our time tomorrow. I said that besides taking her out for an hour tomorrow there were other things I wanted to talk with her about.

I was sure she was questioning the place to which she was going; that her change in residence would come about the day after tomorrow. I wondered whether she would like to know something about the place to which she was going. Elaine shyly smiled and said that she would. I told her about the physical setup; the name, which she thought was a very nice name; about the sewing classes, the school, the activities in the institution, and so on. Elaine said that she could crochet; that she is now making a washcloth. She was interested in the sewing class. She was also interested in the toys. Elaine said that she could ride a bicycle and could skate. She liked to cook and the idea of helping in the cottages appealed to her. She told me some of the things she could cook and was very pleased that she could make quite fancy dishes. She was interested in the library at the institution and said that she had previously belonged to a library. She asked about the ages of the children there, about the cottage mothers, and so on.

I said that the whole idea of this institution must be very new to Elaine. I was sure she couldn't think of all the questions she would like to ask now. However, I would leave her a pencil and paper and she could write down all the questions that came to her mind. When I saw her the following day we could go over the list of questions. Elaine seemed very pleased with this — I thought more pleased because of the fact that she was keeping something tangible to remind her that I was real, than the fact that she would be able to ask questions. (This was confirmed, I thought, the next day when I came. Elaine left the paper and pencil upstairs although she remembered all the questions in her head.) When I left her Elaine squeezed my hand and became very cheerful when she said she would see me the following day and be dressed and ready to go out for a walk.

The following day I met Elaine at the Children's Detention Home. She was all dressed in her own clothes and ready to go out. When I first came she was smiling very broadly and ran to meet me. Although her clothes were torn and patched she presented a rather dignified little appearance. She took my hand immediately and held it tightly throughout the hour we spent together.

Elaine confided to me that she had spent some time trying to make her hair look attractive. (Each morning the matron goes through the dormitory combing everybody's hair with the same comb. There are no mirrors in the Home and the children are not permitted to comb their own hair.)

Elaine had planned the hour in this way: She first wanted to walk in the sunshine, then she wanted to go to a department store and look at the toys. It was interesting to watch Elaine change from a rather dignified, stiff, little girl into a prancing, happy child. She fairly danced after she got used to me and the freedom and the fresh air. When she was ready, we went to the department store that she selected and immediately up to the toy department. When we entered the store Elaine looked at me rather coyly and said that she would like to start with the boys' side first. She was interested in most of the boys' toys, particularly in an electric train. With a rather cute smile and a flirtatious glance she said, "In my neighborhood I'm known as quite a tomboy." When we finished the boys' side and went to the girls' side, Elaine was much less interested. Occasionally she would comment on a doll saying that she had one like it or her sister had one like it. On the whole, she was not interested in the girls' toys. On the way out of the store we stopped at a fountain to get a drink. Elaine had a pineapple soda with chocolate ice-cream, which she drank with a good deal of gusto, getting every last drop out of the glass.

During the hour we were able to talk a little bit about the institution and occasionally she would see a toy and ask whether they had one like it there. Elaine was also able to get from me the details of what would be happening to her the following day in court. I explained that I would not be there since I had to be at the institution on that day. However, since I would be at the institution I would therefore have an opportunity to tell them about her so that they would be expecting her when she came. I gave her a brief description of the people she would meet when she first got there.

When we got back to the Detention Home, Elaine said that the hour had passed all too fast. When I got ready to leave she thanked me and looked up at me with a sort of questioning look. I leaned over and the child put both arms around my neck and kissed me. She then turned her face away and giggled. I gave her a reassuring smile, squeezed her hand, and she went upstairs with the matron.

Elaine comes to life for us in the interviewer's vivid portrayal. The description reveals a discerning observation of a child. In all adequate interviewing, even as the external greetings are taking place, internal mental notes are being made. The worker's first activity is always guided by his early observations. Here the worker immediately sees a frightened, bewildered child. As a result, she takes the initiative, for she realizes that a child precipitated into such a bewildering situation would feel lost, anxious, and insecure in the face of an unknown future. Having been plunged into an unfamiliar detention home, not knowing from day to day what may happen to her, Elaine feels completely at the mercy of grown-ups. She is filled with a sense of futility and helplessness in the face of their overpowering strength and authority.

In addition to realizing all this, the case worker is led to take the initiative because Elaine has not asked for an interview and has no idea why she is being sought out. The worker, therefore, attempts to put the child at ease by telling her at once why she has come, thus free-

94

ing her as much as possible from her natural fear of another new and perhaps calamitous experience. The worker indicates that she wants to be Elaine's friend, something a child can understand. She lets Elaine know also that she understands how Elaine feels about the Detention Home and the uncertainty as to what will happen to her.

One important aspect of the interview consists in allowing the child to express—what she had been unable to mention with others—her dislike of the Detention Home and her unhappiness there. Another is the worker's attempt to visualize as simply and concretely as possible for Elaine what she may expect in the new home to which she will be going. As concrete evidence to the child of her friendliness, she arranges to take her out of the Home for an hour and promises to let Elaine choose how they shall spend that time. If Elaine had not been given any opportunity to talk against the Detention Home, she might have had to bottle up her resentment. By expressing herself, she "gets it off her chest." Further, the very fact of the worker's sympathetic understanding makes it possible for Elaine to regard her many recent troubles as less intolerably unjust.

Although the worker takes the initiative in this interview, it is initiative of a quite different sort from that taken by the court in placing her in the Detention Home without any explanation. The initiative of the worker stimulates Elaine to participate in the plans being made. It is valuable for even a young child to have some feeling that he has a share in important decisions about his own future. It may not be possible to allow Elaine to choose, for instance, whether she will remain with her mother or live away from home, whether she will live in an institution or a foster home, or to choose the institution or foster home in which to live. These are areas in which the agency must take the responsibility for her protection and use its better judgment. Elaine would have no basis on which to make such choices. One cannot make a free choice unless one knows what the alternatives are. In the face of these necessary limitations, the worker arranges for an hour's walk during which Elaine will be completely free to determine what they shall do. An ingenious worker will always find some areas in which she can leave decisions to her client stimulating him to initiative and independent choice and giving him the feeling that he still has some control of the situation.

Here, the worker does what she can also to let Elaine participate as much as possible in the plans being made for her. She is encouraged to talk about them wherever she has enough interest and knowledge to do so. The worker offers to answer such questions about the new home, for instance, as come to Elaine's mind, but she does not volunteer information beyond Elaine's present interests or ken.

Elaine might have asked, for instance, "Will they want a little girl like me who has been bad?" In that instance, the worker might have talked with her further about her experience with her stepfather, but since Elaine did not bring these up, the worker did not push her at this time. Undoubtedly Elaine will need to talk with someone about the experiences which she has had, but if the worker had at such an early point indicated any need to have Elaine talk about these things, Elaine might well have felt that it was indiscreet to discuss such things so soon with a stranger.

The worker implies by her attitude that she understands and that she wants to help, and that there will be others in the new home who will help. Her acceptance of the child's resentment against the Detention Home gives Elaine some security by showing her that there are understanding people in the world with whom one may talk. The worker's sensitive observation of the child's slightest expression is indicated in her recognition of Elaine's desire to kiss her and the worker's unembarrassed response to this. Because Elaine was a frightened, friendless child, this expression of affection from a new friend was natural.

The concrete purpose of this interview was to prepare Elaine to be emotionally ready to accept a new home so that she could go into it with some feeling of security. This was especially important here, because Elaine's many unfortunate experiences would otherwise have led her to expect the worst from another sudden change thrust upon her. This attitude in turn would have jeopardized the success of her placement. This danger was lessened by the interviewer's leading Elaine to look forward with hope to going to her new home.

XIV.

"It's Too Soon"

THE following timely interview, from the Psychiatric Social Work Unit of a state selective service headquarters, shows how the necessarily rigid demands of the Army can be softened by sensitive interviewing in cases where they otherwise would strike with undue harshness.

[George Campbell was referred to the Psychiatric Social Work Unit of a selective service headquarters by an examining psychiatrist. The social worker knew only that the psychiatrist had some question about whether the boy should be deferred. She cleared with the Social Service Exchange and with the State Department of Probation and Mental Health, and found that no social agencies except the school clinic had known the family. The clinic's record indicated that George was one of a large family, that most of the children had been tested, and all had low normal intelligence.

With this scanty information, and without a clear idea of just what specific information would be most helpful to the psychiatrist, she wrote asking the boy to come in.]

George Campbell arrived at the appointed time, came into the draft board headquarters where men were being interviewed, and, instead of addressing himself to the board member who was free, leaned against the counter and waited. When asked if he had come regarding a change in status, he said he had been sent for. I was sitting nearby, and at this point I introduced myself and suggested we go into the adjoining room where we could talk in privacy.

He was a slender, nice-looking fellow, boyishly shy, but covering up his lack of ease with a grin. He stood politely until I invited him to sit down. I said he probably didn't know what I wanted to see him about. He thought maybe I could tell him whether he was going into the Army or not. I said I supposed he was pretty anxious to know. I said he had been temporarily deferred until a social worker could talk with him a little further and we could get more of an idea of how he would fit into the Army. Some men made better soldiers than others. He asked if I would be able to tell him when I got through talking with him if he would have to serve. I said I was afraid I couldn't do even that. My job was to make a report to the draft board and they would take this into consideration along with the facts they already had. He just said, "Oh, that's the way it is. Well, what do you want to know?"

I then directed the conversation to a discussion of jobs he has held, school progress, health history, and family relationships. Throughout he spoke in a rather flat slow voice, mostly only in answer to questions, and with little initiative or spontaneity.

I learned that he had held his present job three and a half months, earned $35 a week, as an unskilled factory hand. This was more money than he had ever earned before, and he would like to keep his job. He thought the family could not get along without his help. His previous work history was irregular except for one job held three and a half years until he was laid off because of the depression.

When I questioned him about school, he said he had gone through two years of high school. How did he get along? He wanted to know what this had to do with it. I said that it would help to know how he got along in other ways. He didn't think school was hard. He just didn't like it. He quit because after ten years it got monotonous. When I asked if he remembered ever having taken an examination given by the school clinic, he shook his head, adding that he knew what the clinic was as they examined twins, but he wasn't a twin. (We had the clinic record of his examination.) I asked if it was all right for me to go to the school to get his academic record. He laughingly said he guessed if the Army wanted it, they would get it anyhow. I said I supposed they would if they wanted to but I did not want to go without his knowing about it. He shrugged and said, "Why should I care? It doesn't make any difference to me."

I referred to his statement about not being a twin and asked about his family. He told me there were ten in his family and that he, an older brother, and his father were working.

I found that there had never been any serious illnesses, and that he had never been in any trouble. He seemed amused when I asked if he had ever been arrested. I turned again to his present situation and asked him how much he understood about his present draft status. He didn't know anything about it except he didn't think it had been decided. I asked how he felt about it—was he anxious to go or just to know? He wasn't very anxious to go: "It's too soon, one is enough for now. It's too soon after losing my brother." I asked if he had lost his brother to the Army too. He looked as if he were going to cry and said his brother lost his life at Pearl Harbor. I said I was awfully sorry to hear that, and asked him to tell me more about it. His brother was younger, eighteen, and had gone into the Navy about a year ago, just as soon as he was old enough. He had always been crazy to join the Navy.

I said this probably affected the way he felt about going. He said naturally he didn't want to go after that. Wouldn't I feel the same? Then, "I guess my brother did my share for me." I said it was hard to realize it when his own brother had been killed, but actually not everyone who went was killed. He said intensely, "But there's plenty that never come back." It was easy to see from his manner that he would not expect to come back and that he was afraid. I said it was natural to feel it was too soon now to go. If he could have some time to get ready, how long would he need? He didn't know. I asked him how his mother felt about his going. "She thinks it's too soon. . . ."

The interview continued for some time while I attempted to re-explore various topics already discussed to make certain that there were no further unrevealed sources of anxiety or other significant material which I might have overlooked. Nothing new turned up, but throughout the balance of the interview I was conscious again and again of the refrain, "It's too soon, one is enough."

In ending the interview, I said I could not give him any decision, but after going to the school I would make a report to the draft board and a letter would come from them. I asked him if they knew about his brother's death and he said he guessed not. Hadn't he told them? "They didn't ask." I told him there was no indication from what he had told me that he could not be a soldier, except that I knew his brother's death had been hard for him and I thought he needed some time to get over it. He just laughed, and then thanked me for seeing him. I wished him good luck whatever the decision was and again he thanked me.

My impression of him was of a slow, inarticulate, compliant boy, relatively shy of intelligence and lacking in initiative and force of his own. He seemed definitely "slowed up," but it was difficult to judge whether this was his usual behavior or a temporary result of the shock of his brother's death and his fear of being drafted.

[Later the worker interviewed George's mother, who corroborated his story in every respect but added no further significant information save a remark, "He doesn't want to be a slacker. Perhaps in six months he'd be ready to go." The school teacher who had known the family for many years reported that none of the children had ever got into trouble but that all had been rather slow in their school work. The worker included in her report to the draft board the recommendation that George be deferred for six months to give him and his family time to recover from the shock of the brother's death.]

In this interview the worker is operating under the handicap of not knowing definitely what information is desired. Thus she doesn't know what specific clues to be on the alert for. In such situations, which are very common, especially in war work, the interviewer must rely on his general knowledge of the characteristic features of human nature and on his mastery of interviewing skill. The boy does not know why he has been called in and the worker is not in a position to give him the usual opening clarification as to the manifest purpose of the interview. She is forced to look farther afield to find some common ground on which the conversation can begin. She explains that the draft board has asked her to find out more about him and his background so that they will be better able to judge how well fitted he would be for army life.

The interviewer is uncertain as to what the psychiatrist had in mind in recommending further investigation. Did he suspect low intelligence, mental instability, delinquency, or what? She doesn't even know at first whether the boy wants deferment or would regret it. Her recourse is to explore various fields, previous employment, health history, school achievement, and family relationships.

Her problem is made even more difficult by the fact that George does not respond readily to usually successful leading questions. He never carries the conversation far under his own initiative. As far as

99

she can tell for a long time, he seems to have nothing "on his mind." By her sustained and varied inquiries the worker finally elicits a revealing response: "It's too soon, one is enough." George proffers a reason for his reluctance to be drafted. That it is basic is shown by his constant reiteration of it once it has been mentioned.

Her general knowledge of the effects of traumatic human experiences and her recognition of the common human need for a "period of mourning" enable the interviewer to understand the stunning effect of the brother's death upon George and his family. She gives him an opportunity to relieve the tenseness of his feeling by talking about the tragedy, but she soon recognizes that in his case "talking will not be enough." She concludes that time is needed to relieve the stress.

XV.
"A Guy Acts Tough So Nobody Knows He's Scared"

THE following interview from a family agency is especially valuable for purposes of study, because, as part of a research project, it was written out fully and almost verbatim. It reveals remarkable skill on the part of the interviewer in speaking the language of his client. It shows also his skill in overcoming an adolescent's distrust and reluctance to talk and in discovering the underlying reasons for behavior that is hard to understand.

[The Ames family, consisting of the parents and five sons, applied to the family agency for advice on meeting threats of garnishments which jeopardized Mr. Ames' part-time job with a milling company.

Both Mr. and Mrs. Ames seemed dull and very much worried about their financial problems. They owed $675 in back bills, principally to loan companies and the company credit union. Bankruptcy proceedings would have cost Mr. Ames his job. Temporary financial assistance was given, and Mr. Ames talked with his creditors and arranged an orderly small payment system of keeping his accounts in good standing. With reduced payments on bills, some assistance from the family agency, and an increase in work, Mr. Ames was able to manage better. When Mrs. Ames was no longer so worried about the bills, she began to talk about other problems.

The parents apparently lacked ability to deal with the problems of the children. When the second oldest son, Wallace, refused to enter school (although he was below compulsory school age), Mrs. Ames asked the worker to see him as she was baffled by the situation and his behavior. The following interview is the first of a number that the case worker had with Wallace.]

Wallace Ames came to the agency office. When he came into the waiting-room, he sat down, his eyes cast down toward the floor. He slouched in his chair and when I said, "Good morning," and that I was glad to see him, he simply nodded his head. I asked him how things turned out over at the University Hospital. (The boy had been going to the hospital to clear up a skin rash.) He grunted, said nothing. There was a pause. I asked him if he had been at the University Hospital the day before and he said, "Yes." "Well, did you see Dr. Martin?" "No, he wasn't there."

Another pause. I went and got the letter which we had received from the University Hospital and handed it to him. He looked it over and said, "I knew it wouldn't do no good to go there, they don't know anything anyhow. They just make you sit around and after awhile some guy tells you that he can't do anything. Then you pay your quarter or maybe you pay the quarter first and then you go home. All they want to do is experiment on people over there and those doctors don't know nothing."

101

"Well, I wouldn't be too sure about that," I said, "after all, generally doctors at a hospital are trying to help people." "Huh, there is nothing that is going to help me, and anyhow I don't care whether they do anything for me or not." "Well, that's all right if you don't want to go over there, I guess that's pretty much up to you. I guess nobody is going to force you to go over there."

At this point, Wallace glanced up very briefly, then continued the gazing at the floor. "You mean you're not going to chase me over there?" "Yes, that's what I mean. I thought it would make it a little easier for you if the doctor was helping you out in getting this breaking-out business cleared up, but that's up to you whether you want to go over there or not."

"Well, having a rash isn't so bad, but there's a lot of other things too." "Yes, I know there are a lot of things that a fellow has to get figured out and sort of face, and I thought maybe you and I could talk things over. Now that is up to you too. If we can be friends and sort of talk together, O.K., if not I won't ask you a lot of questions."

This first section represents the attempt of the worker and Wallace to get together. Each is sounding out the other, the boy suspiciously, the worker sympathetically.

Interviewing an adolescent has special difficulties of its own. Adolescents, more even than most human beings, are torn by confusions and uncertainties. Wallace illustrates one of the outstanding characteristics of adolescents. They are often dominated by the feeling that others don't understand them. They keep their thoughts to themselves, become secretive, harbor and exaggerate their secrets, and are convinced that they would be laughed at or misunderstood if they talked. Actually such an attitude reflects their own inability to understand themselves. They project on to others their own lack of understanding. Further, they are often so successful in withholding their feelings that they do indeed make themselves inscrutable to persons trying to help them. Wallace does both these things.

In this interview the worker was confronted by a pretty definite determination of the boy not to talk, and there was no simple easy way to get beyond this point. Sometimes interviews bog down at this stage over the abstract issue: to talk or not to talk. The sooner the interview can be shifted to a discussion of some concrete problem the better. Of course, in the beginning, the problem raised must not be such as to arouse the fears of the client, for this would simply confirm his determination to remain silent. It is sometimes difficult to find a relevant field where the client can talk freely. Here the interviewer engages in considerable preliminary fencing before succeeding in getting Wallace to talk.

In studying the early part of this interview, we are a little handicapped because we do not know exactly what Wallace had been told about coming in for this appointment. If he had had no explanation at all, it would seem natural for the worker to have begun the interview with some such explanation as occurs at the end of the first section. Such an early explanation might have given Wallace at the beginning some reassurance as to what the worker's attitude would be so that he would have needed to maintain his barriers a little less long.

The worker does begin with something concrete—Wallace's visit to the hospital. This is at least a safe start, serving as a trial balloon to see how the boy will respond. Actually he talks fairly freely about the hospital. The worker's response, "Well, I wouldn't be too sure about that," falls into the boy's argumentative mood, and with hindsight one can see that it might have been better to have accepted more completely how the boy felt about going to the hospital, with some such comment as, "Yes, it is pretty discouraging to sit around waiting for doctors and then not have them tell you very much," and then to have followed this later with the worker's concluding comment that doctors really do want to help people though it may not always seem that way when they don't seem able to help right away.

The worker's comment, "Well, that's all right if you don't want to go over there," surprises Wallace, as it deprives him of one issue he had expected to fight about. The worker's intentions here are obvious, to assure the boy that he will not be forced to do something that he does not want to, that it is his own decision to make. In giving clients assurances of this sort, interviewers should be on their guard lest such comments assume too much a "take it or leave it" attitude. "It's all up to you" is sometimes interpreted by the client not as allowing him self-determination but as reflecting a half-hearted interest on the part of the worker. Here the interviewer's following comment, "I thought it would make it a little easier for you if the doctor was helping you out," expresses his interest and allays the other impression which might have been given by his insistence that it was all up to Wallace. Wallace's comment, "Well, having a rash isn't so bad, but there's a lot of other things too," gives the worker early in the interview the clue that Wallace does have things on his mind which are troubling him and which he is consciously aware of.

The worker's insistence that he is not going to ask a lot of questions is good, because it allays what is obviously Wallace's anticipatory fear of the procedure.

There was a long pause. Wallace said, "You know my mother and father, don't you?" "Yes, I do know them." "Well, the old man, he has been trying to get his bills paid, so we haven't any clothes, and we aren't on relief so we can't get stamps and things like a lot of people can." I told Wallace, "I know your father is and has been doing a lot about getting his bills fixed up, and I think he has done a good job of it. So has your mother and I guess you kids had to pitch in too, and you helped out by being willing to go without having a lot of things you might have wanted." He considered this for a moment and said, "Oh, yeah, well, you don't know the half of it."

There was a pause. I thought he was going to go on and say more, but he did not. I said, "Well, I guess probably I don't know all about it and I wonder if you want to talk with me about it." "It wouldn't do any good." "Maybe it wouldn't and maybe it would, that's up to you." "I thought you were just going to ask me a lot of questions." "No," I paused deliberately. "You see, Wally, I want to be your friend, but I don't want to, as I told you before, force myself into this. You and I can talk like one fellow to another. You can say whatever you want to say. I know there are a lot of things that you wonder about, probably a lot of things that make you sort of sore. If you want to talk to me about those things, you go ahead. If you don't want to talk about them, forget it. I understand." He looked at me directly for a moment and then gazed at the floor. There was what seemed to be an almost interminable pause.

Then he said, "Well, gee, there are a lot of things that I don't know it would do any good to say anything about. You better talk with my mother or somebody because what's the use of me talking?" I said, "Look, Wally, you're the fellow I'm trying to talk to now. I figure what happens to you and how you feel about things are important, and what you say means just as much as what your mother or your father would say. You seem to me to be pretty sore about something and you are keeping it inside of yourself. Sometimes it does help if we come out and say what's on our mind." "Yeah, I suppose it does, but what good would it do?" "Well, maybe it would help to say it and then, too, maybe working along together we could figure some of these things out. I understand that you don't want to go back to school and I guess that that's worrying your mother and father some, and I wonder if you want to talk about that." Another pause. "It wouldn't do any good." "Maybe not and then again it might." The boy looked at me for a moment, then said, "All I want to do is to go to Vocational High School, you don't learn anything up at Sheridan."

Wallace now seems to be making a real effort to "talk," assigning his difficulty to their poverty. The worker's "I guess you kids had to pitch in too" goes beyond what Wallace has said and expresses the worker's understanding and appreciation of what Wallace has done. Wallace again refers vaguely to "You don't know the half of it." The worker agrees that he doesn't know about it, but, "I wonder if you want to talk with me about it." This is met with Wallace's stubborn refusal, "It wouldn't do any good," and again the worker slips into what sounds like an argumentative statement, "Maybe it wouldn't and maybe it would, that's up to you." The worker's tone of voice and facial expression would determine whether it was argumentative or not. Similarly the tone of "That's up to you" would indicate to the client whether the worker was giving Wallace freedom of decision or was simply washing his hands of the matter. It would, of course, have been unwise for the worker to make any false promises at this point that he was sure that he could help.

The worker's explanation of wanting to be his friend and to "talk like one fellow to another" breaks through some of Wallace's suspicion, and leads him to express his desire to go to Vocational High School. This represents the first real movement in the interview. Now it can proceed to more specific topics.

He waited for me to make some comment, and I said, "I think it's a good idea if you want to go down to Vocational High School. What do you want to take down there?" A much shorter pause, "Oh, I would like to take woodwork, I got an A in my woodwork up at school and I'd like to take more of that." "Well, that sounds fine to me. What kind of things did you make?" "Oh, I made an end-table and I made a floor lamp, no, it was a desk lamp, that had over two hundred pieces of wood in it." "Well, tell me a little bit about it."

He then, with a sudden freeing of reserve, talked for a couple of minutes, telling me about some of the details of the construction of his lamp and ended up by saying, "And I took it home and my mother thought it was swell and my father said it was done better than a lot of carpenters that he knew could do." "Well, that was swell, Wally, and it is fun to build something nice, isn't it?" "It sure is but then I guess I'll never get into Vocational High School. Anyhow, you got to have a drag to get in there."

"Well, I'm not too sure about the drag side of it. Maybe we could work with and help you get lined up so you could get into that school. One thing I do know is that you have to complete the ninth grade before you can get in now." "I haven't finished the ninth grade yet and it doesn't look like I'm going to get to go to school any more unless I can get clothes and stuff because I ain't going to go to school when I haven't got any clothes to wear." "Is that the reason you don't want to go back to school now?" "Well, I haven't got any shoes and the only pants that I have got are overall pants. I earned the money this summer helping a guy fix the siding on his house. Then I bought some pants for myself, but they are not good enough to go to school. Most of the stuff I have, my older brother wore first and I just don't like it and I'm not going to go to school." This last was said in a most defiant sort of tone, and the boy seemed to close up.

He stared off into space, and I noticed that his hands were clenched and that he was red in the face. I said, "I don't blame you for feeling sort of unhappy about that, probably there is some way we can get around that; I think that if you want to go down to Vocational bad enough, it's like earning your way to go down there to get your ninth grade finished up, and you do have to have that before you can get in." "Well, I suppose so, so I guess it's just like happens to a lot of fellows, you know what you want but you can't get it." "I guess you have to work pretty hard, and I guess all of us have to work pretty hard to get the things that we want." "Sure, that's O.K., but it isn't going to do any good for me."

"Well, maybe it can be worked out." "No, it can't. My dad hasn't got no money and we can't ask for any help any place, and I haven't even got any shoes that will do to wear." At this point, he held up his foot and showed me that he was wearing a very heavy, high-top shoe which looked very stiff and uncomfortable. The boy flushed painfully and continued, "It isn't like my dad could help it or anything, 'cause he doesn't lose or throw away his money foolish like a lot of guys do, but he just doesn't make enough so that we can get along right. He promised that he would get me some shoes, but then they started chasing him on the bills and all he could do was to get these shoes fixed, and I can't do anything about it."

I had the feeling that the boy was fairly close to tears at this point and said, "Wally, I think you're a pretty good boy. You understand what your father is up against." "Well, it isn't his fault anyhow, and I can't be sore at him, but a guy can't go to school and sit in a room full of girls and everything when he hasn't got the pants that are right or anything and then his face looks all funny, and they don't let you take Commercial Math like you want to."

"What's this business about Commercial Math?" "Well, there were some guys in the class that were going to take Commercial Math and I wanted to take Commercial Math but they said I had to take Algebra. They wouldn't let me change and take what I wanted to take. You're supposed to have three subjects that you can take what you want to and they would not let me take Commercial Math."

The boy said this with real vehemence and when I looked questioningly, he went on to say, "I wouldn't have made any trouble if I had been with these other guys, but I don't see why I should be the one who had to sit in the class with a bunch of girls where you couldn't talk or anything." "Well, that does seem sort of unfair, but after all, if the school people say something, sometimes you just can't get them to change their minds, and I guess we have to put up with things in order to get it fixed so we can finish the ninth grade and get down to Vocational if that's what you're going to do."

"Yeah, well, it's easy to say that but just the same I don't like it and I'm not going back up there now." "Well, that happened last quarter. Do you think the same thing is going to happen again during this fall?" "Well, I don't know. I haven't been up there." "Right there, Wally, I think that you are saying you won't go to school on account of the classes they want you to take, but you don't know what the classes are they are going to ask you to take."

He paused, thought that over and continued, "Maybe you're right there, but there are other things. The doctors, they can't do my face any good and I still haven't got clothes and that isn't all there is." "Well, do you like the people that you see around school?" "Oh, most of the boys are all right." "How do you get along with the teachers and so on?" "Oh, I get along pretty good with most of them." "Do you get fairly good grades?" "Sure, when I work I get good grades. I'm as smart as any of them, but I just don't care about it. They don't teach you anything. You hear it all on the first day and then it's the same stuff every day." "Maybe that's so, but somehow I think that by the time you've been attending a class for three or four months that probably you do know more than when you went into it." "Well, maybe that's so, but it doesn't seem like it to me."

"You said that there were some other things too." "Yeah, but you wouldn't understand them." "I would try to understand them and I guess I can't understand them unless you tell me about them, can I?" "No, you can't."

"As I said to you before, it's up to you, Wally, how much you want to say, and what you want to talk about. Is something still kind of bothering you? I'm sorry, but I'm not going to ask you a lot more questions. In summing up what we have been talking about here, you figure you haven't got the right kind of clothing to go to school and I guess probably that you've got some real reason to feel that way. Probably we can work something out with your folks about that. I do think that if you want to go to Vocational High School that we would try to help you in making a plan to get in down there. But, of course, it's up to you in getting the ninth grade out of the way. Also, if we can work with you in getting this business over at the hospital fixed up, maybe some doctor can do something, but as a matter of fact, as far as I can see, your face looks perfectly O.K. to me, and I think for a guy as grown up as you are that you're making an awful lot out of something that probably other people don't notice as much as you think they do." With that I picked up the letter from the University Hospital and made some motions as though I were going to terminate the interview.

Again the worker introduces reality by pointing out the things which Wallace can change and those which he can't. "Sometimes you've just got to do what the school people say." But again he points out that Wally is refusing to go to school on the basis of something that happened last year without having found out what courses he might be allowed to take this year.

From Wallace's repeated remark, "That isn't all there is," the worker infers that there is a more basic difficulty that has not yet come to the surface. He attempts to bring this to light by specific questions about the boys at school, the teachers, and Wallace's grades. Since none of these questions lead to what Wallace was obviously hinting at, the worker decides that the discovery of this will have to wait until later, and he sums up the interview and moves to terminate it.

The boy stood up as though he were going to leave, turned around, and said, "Well, there are some other things too. There are some kind of private things that, gee, I maybe could tell you about but I don't know whether I should or not." "Well, that's up to you. I'd be glad to talk over anything you want to talk about. I know that it is kind of hard to talk, so maybe you'd like to come in sometime again and talk."

The boy went to the door, turned around, came back, and said, "Well, I sort of thought you were going to ask me a lot of questions and everything, and you didn't do it, and I guess it was all right for me to come in." "I'm glad you came in and remember the door is open if you want to come in again. I guess that I haven't helped you very much, but I can't do much if anybody doesn't want to go along with me, you know." "Yes, I guess I understand that."

There was an awkward pause for a moment, the boy went and sat down again, and said, "You won't tell my mother about this because she'd be upset and it would make my dad feel bad if they knew everything I told you." "Of course, I won't tell them all that you say because there are a lot of things that we don't need to talk over with them. There will be some things that, of course, I will want to talk with them about."

"Well, it's this way. I'm pretty sore at the school but I still want to go back down to school so I can go to Vocational High School, and I'm going to go back to school and then I will get into Vocational, but that isn't all. I feel so silly when I go up there to school."

"Well, if it is the clothing matter, I guess there is some way we can get around that." "It isn't just the pants and the shoes and the jacket I haven't got, I got underwear that I can't take my pants off in school, and, oh, gee, you'd laugh if I tell you now what it is." His sentence was all jumbled up and the boy was acutely uncomfortable. I said, "No, I won't laugh, Wally, because I know that sometimes there are little things that happen that just hurt like the dickens." "Well, what I was trying to tell you was that the underwear that I have hasn't any opening in front like a man's underwear has, and it's cut off old woman's underwear, and when I go down to the toilet room the guys see me and they laugh at me, and I have to kind of go sneaking in and then when it's gym time, I gotta change my clothes, and—" the boy was almost on the verge of tears; in fact, there were tears in his eyes, and he stammered and came to a halt, and I said, "Of course, that is tough, and I know it. I'm glad you told me about it because it does help me to understand."

He went on, "And then on my arm sometimes it shows this rash, sometimes on my back, and the guys say that I got a dose of something, and that isn't so, or they make some crack about my old man having had something, and gee, whiz, I can't stand it." The boy began to cry, rather half-sobbing, and he buried his face in his hands.

"Wally, that is too bad, and I really am sorry. Now, instead of giving up because some fellows have made cracks, let's figure out what to do, so we can get you back where you want to go to school and get you built up so you will have a better chance to go to Vocational."

The boy with a rather quick gesture wiped his eyes, and I continued, "Wally, you had real courage when you told me about that, and I know it was hard to say these things, but any fellow that's got courage enough to talk that way has the stuff to meet it, that is, to get things figured out and worked on. Now, let's put our heads together and take this thing a step at a time. I know you can't tell your mother about the underwear business." He interrupted me, "She'd feel real bad because she knows that we haven't any money to get underwear."

"That's right, but maybe if she got the idea, she could take some old material that she might have around and make you some shorts. I've seen that done a lot of times." "You think she could do that?" "Sure, she could do that. I know she is a good sewer." "Yes, she is a good sewer. She makes a lot of things over and I don't mind wearing stuff that's made over, but it's got to be like the other guys wear." "Of course, it does. Would you object to my just suggesting to her how she could make some underwear over for you that would be like regular shorts?" "Gee, do you think you could do it without her knowing or feeling bad about it?" "Yes, I think I could do it. Now if we could lick that underwear problem, that would help some there, wouldn't it?" "Sure, it would."

"Well, now let's see about this clothes business. What do you think it would cost to get some pants, shoes, and a jacket?" "Oh, I don't know. It wouldn't do any good anyhow because they haven't got the money, and I don't want to have a row about it so I'm just not going to go to school." "Now, there you go, Wally, slipping right back where you were. I thought we were going to work together on this." "Well, there is just nothing that can be done." "No, there isn't anything that can be done if you won't go along with it." "Well, what do you think you can do. Do you think you can fix it with the old man so that he can get some stuff?"

"I might have to talk with him about that, but first I think we need to know how much it's going to cost for this stuff. How about your going and finding out how much these things would cost." "No, I couldn't do that." "Why not?" "Well, I never did that before." "No, well, all right, now is a good time to start. Maybe you could figure it out and give me the facts on it and then we'd know what we were talking about when we talked with the folks." "Well, if you think so."

"Wally, it isn't just what I think, it's how you think about it. After all, you're growing up and when you're working on your own, you'll have to do this buying for yourself." "Well, I hadn't thought about it that way." "There is no time like now to start to get things on your own figuring and planning, is there?" "No, I guess not." "Didn't you tell me a little while ago that you bought yourself a pair of pants this summer with money that you earned?" "Well, yes, but that was different." "How do you mean that?" "Well, that was just one pair of pants, but this is big stuff." "Yes, I know it's big stuff, and it is quite a responsibility, but I do think you can go to the store and find out what the prices would be." "Well, I guess I'll do that then."

I continued, "Your mother was planning to come in tomorrow morning and if I have the amount of what it would cost, maybe I could talk that over with her then." "Yes, you could do that, but I don't know whether I could find out how much things would cost before then." "Well, that's up to you. Excepting the sooner you get back to school, the better it's going to be, and incidentally, you're still under sixteen, and the school people are going to be looking to see what's become of you if you don't get back there pretty quick." "Yeah, I know that, and I don't want to have any trouble with anybody because when they once get it in for you then you are in a bad spot." "Yes, I agree with you. It is smarter not to let anybody get it in for you."

The boy hesitated for a moment and then said, "I'd better tell you before somebody else does, that I got into trouble once." "Oh, did you?" "Yes, but it wasn't near as bad as they made it out to be. They said that I'd been snitching some stuff so I got put on probation. I went down there every week. They only saw you for about two minutes, then sent you home again. All they did was to make you run back and forth and it didn't amount to nothing. They just try to show you that they are the boss."

109

"You were on probation then?" "Yes, I was, but my brother, he got in worse trouble and he was worse off than I was." "That's too bad, but you haven't been in any trouble since then, have you?" "No, and I'm not going to get in any trouble any more either because they get it in for you and then you're in an awful lot of trouble all of the time."

I told him that he had a pretty practical point of view on that and the boy smiled and went on to say, "You really think if I got my clothes fixed up and got right back to school quick that I could get into Vocational?" "Well, I can't promise that they'd let you in because there have to be vacancies for people, but you sure wouldn't get in until you get the ninth grade completed, and I guess that that's the first thing for you to do, that's the only smart move."

"Yes, I guess that it is, and, say, you won't tell anybody about the things that I told you, now will you?" "Of course I won't." "Maybe I'm just getting made a sap out of talking like this." "You really think that, Wally?" "Well, no, but I've known guys that have talked to people and told them a lot of things and then they have gone and rat on them." "Do you think that I would rat on you, Wally?" "Well, no," he said this rather hesitantly. "Wally, what have I got to gain by talking to you and then spreading it around?" "Well, I don't suppose you get anything." "All right, now do you think I would rat on you?" "No, I guess not, but I never talked to anybody that I hadn't known for a long time and practically never talked to anybody really like I have been telling you about my underwear and things."

"I know that, and I know it wasn't easy for you, and maybe after a while you'll wonder why you told me those things. Well, don't worry about it. That was just between us and because I thought that if you told me those things it would make it easier for you to go back to school. Now do you understand?" "I guess I do." "I'm glad that you came back, Wally, when we were ready to stop talking the first time, and now that we have, have you got it pretty clear what you're going to do?" "Sure I have. I'm going to find out what the prices would be and then you're going to get it fixed up with my folks as soon as you can about some clothes so I can get back and go to school."

"All right, will you be coming in with your mother tomorrow?" "Oh, I don't know whether I will or not, but I'll come in and see you some time again, maybe." "That's up to you, Wally. I know when you're going to school it isn't so easy, but pretty generally if I know someone wants to see me I'm here Saturday morning. How about next Saturday morning?" "Well, maybe, only I'd like to kind of see about a job so I can work some while I'm going to school."

"Say, that's a good idea—for Saturdays or something like that, you mean?" "Yeah, but there isn't much chance to get a job. I tried to get a paper route once, but I couldn't get no bond and there wasn't any routes around close by. You gotta have a lot of pull if you're going to get something like that."

"Pull, what do you mean?" "Well, I went to a meeting where they were going to fix up some paper routes, but the guy that was there told me that I had a chip on my shoulder and that you couldn't get any place acting like that so I just figured that some guy that was making up to this fellow would get the job so I didn't do anything more about it. It wouldn't do any good anyhow."

"Well, Wally, it seems to me that maybe that newspaper fellow had something there when he said you had a chip on your shoulder. Several things you said here sounded that way to me but really I wonder if maybe you don't act that way because you're kind of covering up a little bit." "You mean that I am sort of scared so I act tough." "You certainly figured that one out in a hurry, Wally, and isn't it true?"

The boy grinned a really amused smile and said, "Gee, you sure got that figured out." "How do you mean that, Wally?" "Well, you know how it is—a guy gets on a spot so he acts tough so nobody knows that he is scared." I told him that that's pretty natural. I guess everybody did it until they learned that when they really could do a job or could get along without acting that it was easier not to act tough. He considered this for a moment and then said, "Well, after I get stuff kind of figured out maybe I'll come in some Saturday morning, but anyhow when my mother comes down tomorrow, why, I'll have talked to her and maybe sometime you'll give me a tip-off about this paper route business."

"There isn't any tip-off that I can give you. There is a man down there by the name of Coolidge that fixed up routes for two or three boys that I've known, and if you talk with him you can tell him that you know me; beyond that I guess there isn't much of a tip-off I can give you. It is up to you to get out and see what you can do." "You mean it would be smart for me to go down there?" "It might be. I don't know that there would be anything, but it never does any harm to look around a little." "Well, I got to think about that."

The interview was running quite long, and so I told him that I was glad he had come in. If he wanted to come in again, fine. I would be looking for information from him through his mother the following morning, and that I would be glad and willing to see him at any time that we could arrange an appointment. I terminated the interview fairly quickly and Wally walked to the door, turned around, and looked at me for a moment, and said, "Well, this isn't what I figured at all." "All right, if I disappointed you I'm sorry, but I really enjoyed talking to you, Wally, and I'll be seeing you." I put out my hand, the boy seized it, and turned and dashed down the hall.

The interview here proceeds to a more realistic discussion of Wallace's difficulties in going to school. He expresses his enthusiasm for woodwork and reveals his desire not to blame his parents.

We note the worker's keen observations of Wallace's body tensions, his clenched hands, flushing, and signs of deep emotion. His general suspicion and tendency to displace his difficulties onto others is revealed by his comment, "You've got to have a drag to get in there." The worker picks this up for a moment but lets it drop at this time and continues to discuss concrete ways in which Wallace can get into Vocational School. The worker continually brings him back to the reality that he must finish the ninth grade before he can go to Vocational School.

The worker is now getting a sense of Wallace's difficulties so that he is able to respond readily with expressions of sympathy: "I don't blame you for feeling sort of unhappy about that," "Well, that does seem sort of unfair." Also his relationship is well enough established so that he can comment appreciatively on Wally's excuses for his father, "Wally, I think you're a pretty good boy," and Wally in turn expresses easily his dilemma—he's "sore" but he doesn't know where to place this soreness, since he knows he cannot blame his father.

The interview proceeds with the worker's being able to pick up clues, "What's this business about Commercial Math?" and at times to secure a response to merely a questioning look.

The worker has now convinced Wallace of his real desire to help and has given him enough specific suggestions to lead him to feel that perhaps his stubborn feeling that nothing can be done is mistaken. Wallace has been hesitating about revealing the distressing situation which has most inhibited him. His realization that the interview is about to terminate precipitates him into a decision to reveal even this. His fear that the worker will laugh at him as do the boys at school for wearing women's underwear is allayed, and he is able to share his "shame." The worker responds understandingly, "Wally, that's too bad, and I really am sorry. Now instead of giving up because some fellows have made cracks, let's figure out what to do so we can get you back where you want to be in school."

They "put their heads together" and Wally is encouraged to feel that the worker will help him at some of the spots that are most difficult, but that he can help himself too by taking part of the responsibility such as in finding out about the prices of clothes. Throughout, the worker builds up Wallace's confidence in himself through expressing his own confidence in Wallace.

Now he brings up what he had refrained from mentioning before for fear of being identified with school authorities, the fact that Wallace really does have to get back to school or the truant officer will be active.

Wallace now feels so much confidence that he changes from being sullen and uncommunicative to wanting to confess and to tell even more than the worker has suggested. Perhaps he wants to be sure that even if the worker knows that he has been in trouble he will still be liked.

Now Wallace is ready to plan ahead about getting a job. Earlier the worker's suggestions that he get a job might have been interpreted

112

by Wallace as prying into his business and trying to force him to do something. Now too when Wallace again says that "you have to have a drag" in order to get a job, the worker is able to pick this up. "Well, Wally, it seems to me that maybe that newspaper fellow had something there when he said that maybe you had a chip on your shoulder. . . . I wonder if maybe you don't act that way because maybe you're kind of covering up a little bit." This interpretation is immediately effective as Wally is able to go on and make his own more complete interpretation, "You mean that I'm sort of scared and so I act tough?" and later, "A guy gets on the spot so he acts tough so no one knows that he's scared." The worker reassures Wally that his behavior is natural but does not imply that it is correct. He doesn't blame him for the feelings that he has but he suggests to him the wisdom of modifying his behavior, not to please the worker, but so that he himself may get along better and be happier.

The unusual length of time required for this interview seems to have been justified. Because of the painful slowness of the beginning, it would have been unfortunate if the worker had had to terminate the interview at the end of a given time rather than wait for the final revealing "confession" about the underwear.

XVI.
"It Makes Sense, But . . ."

IN closing we turn again to fiction. The following two interviews are selected from Phyllis Bottome's *London Pride*.[1]

The story centers around a seven-year-old cockney Londoner, Ben Barton, during the early days of the war. He is one of six children of a dockworker. Mrs. Barton is a charwoman. Bert and Flossie, adolescents, are white collar workers, with whom Ben has relatively little contact. The twins, Alfred and Vi'let, ten years old, are "strong and familiar enemies" of Ben. The baby, Mabel, two years old, is "Ben's very own."

In our first selection the author describes Ben's introspection as he listens to an interview between his mother and "the Vision." The Vision has come to persuade his mother to evacuate her children.

Lurking well under the kitchen table, where he had safely secluded himself, without his mother's or her visitor's being aware of his presence, Ben listened with the careful suction of a vacuum cleaner, and drew down into himself, for future sorting, anything of direct interest let fall either by the visitor or his mother.

The visitor smelt like a flower shop and looked like a large golden fruit upon a kitchen plate. . . . Ben gathered that his mother did not consider this delectable Vision wholly in the light of an enemy . . . He saw that his mother felt uneasy, but only because she didn't want to do what the Lady suggested should be done—and yet didn't like saying that she wouldn't do it. . . .

"You've no idea," the Lady went on persuasively, "what a comfort it *is* to know that your children are safe! I *do* know how hard it is to part with them, because you see I've parted with my own! I've sent them to Canada. I shan't see them till the war is over; but I know that they are safe! Yours would be nearly as safe in this country—without having to cross the sea either—if you'd let them be evacuated. You could go with them yourself if you preferred, as your youngest is only a year old, and the Government will help you financially. . . .

"They'll be so clean and healthy in that lovely air," the Voice went on after a pause for inspection [of Mabel]. "I promise you they'll find a really good home for the children—and for you and Baby as well, if you decide to go with them."

"And wot's ter 'appen to Mr. Barton and my Bert and Flossie while I'm away?" Mrs. Barton sharply demanded. " 'E's as good a 'usband as if 'e wasn't one! 'E brings in all 'e orter of wot 'e gets. 'E 'as to 'ave somethink for 'is beer, 'is fags and 'is papers, 'asn't 'e? . . . My 'usband expects 'is meals and 'is home,

---

[1] Material reprinted by special permission of Little, Brown and Company, Boston.

114

for wot 'e brings in—an' it's only right 'e should 'ave 'em! My two eldest—they give what they 'ave to according to the Law. But their 'ome's their 'ome, Gov-ern-mint or no Govern-mint—an' the little things they get done for 'em— well, I am their muvver, ain't I? It's only fair I should give 'em a 'elping 'and now an' again—whether they need it or not!"

Mrs. Barton became suddenly belligerent. She felt vaguely that her mater-nity was being attacked by this strange Lady who sent her children across a sea invaded by German submarines. Who was she, to give advice or reproof to a mother who would have died where she stood to have saved her children from such a risk, and her own heart from such a parting?

"But it's to keep them *safe!*" the Lady pleaded, as if she read the sharp protest in Mrs. Barton's mind.

Ben had never seen anyone with so much sympathy before. She seemed sparkling with virtues bred from early morning teas, the use of daily baths, and deep comfortable armchairs. She was soft, but she was also kind and good. Only she didn't know what partings meant when you couldn't afford journeys, or telegrams, or even too many stamps. . . . Ben had spent a day once at the seaside—a crammed, succulent, exhausting day.

Now, he might have to go again, for an indefinite period—not to return tri-umphantly in the evening to the familiar friendly smell of his own street where he could boast of the day's adventures to an admiring and envious world.

If he went now, he would have to stay in a strange empty place—without a home to come back to—even perhaps without his mother or Mabel. . . .

[The Vision went on, "There will be] fields full of cows, and lambs—or perhaps the sea! We were thinking of Devon or Cornwall . . . for this next batch. I'm quite sure the children will love it!"

"Coo!" Ben said [emerging from beneath the table]. "Coo—'ow'd yer know we'd love it? *You* ain't our muvver!"

The apricot Lady hesitated. After all, was she so sure what this undersized, lean and dirty shaveling, with his intelligent eyes and mysterious habits, would be likely to love?

She was really a kind-hearted woman, and tears sprang to her eyes—for she knew that a child of seven ought *not* to look like a midget of seventy.

"You'll be so free," she ventured after a pause, "and you'll have heaps of good nourishing food. There'll be rocks and cliffs—and birds in the hedges. When the summer comes you'll be able to swim and paddle on the beach!"

Ben made a gesture with his thumb in the direction of the Docks. "We got the river any'ow," he told her. Still, he was impressed. Mabel had never been to the seaside or the country. . . .

[Ben] realized that his mother had made up her mind. She wouldn't go from London. She was rooted, she and Ben and Mabel. Ben lifted the table-cloth and met her eyes, signaling to her his deep complicity. She might count on him. He would give up the country for Mabel and himself without undue reluctance. Such vast nameless spaces were all right for those that liked them; but where were the streets—the shops—the Docks? Where were the noises, the smells, the fatal accidents, the hairbreadth escapes? What was life without the jostled sensations of humanity?

The apricot Lady said reasonably, "You will have to think it over, of course, and consult with your husband. I'll leave all the Forms for you to show him. You see, we can't expect—since France has fallen—that we can prevent London from being bombed; and bombed cities are no place for children, Mrs. Barton! Try to take my word for it. They will be in dreadful danger!"

"Well—there was all that talk last September when the war began," explained Mrs. Barton apologetically, " 'alf our neighbours *did* send their children orf, but 'Itler never *as* bombed nothing—except down the river 'ere and there! An' when the children came back—which most of 'em in our street 'ave done by now—granted they looked better an' 'ealthier, but that's all worn off— they didn't get on so well in their own 'omes as they used to! Always turning up their noses at things they was satisfied wiv before! Wot I says is, 'Let yer children go away onct—an' they comes back strangers!' "

Mrs. Barton spoke with spirit, but not in actual condemnation of this other mother who had let her children go—as far away even as to Canada. Poor little mites, she thought, driven out across the haunted seas! But the Lady meant well by them no doubt. With ladies it was different. Their children would only go to places where there were other ladies to take care of them. They would still have all their old comforts and securities; but once let *her* children go, Mrs. Barton told herself fiercely, and anything might happen to them.

"I'll think it over," she agreed, wiping her hands on her apron, "and I know you mean kindly. . . . Flossie, that's my eldest girl, she's a good child of course, but yer don't leave 'em at seventeen if you can 'elp it. I don't interfere with 'er now she earns 'er own money, in a manner of speaking. But I *do* know when she comes in of an evening—and 'oo she goes abaht wiv! An' my old man— well I ain't ever left 'im before. Nor you don't know what goin's-on 'usbands mightn't be up to behind your back, do you?"

"But this bombing," the Lady pleaded—"it's a matter of life and death, you know, Mrs. Barton—an Air War is so terribly *dangerous!*"

"Lots of things is dangerous if it comes ter that!" said Mrs. Barton tolerantly. " 'Itler's only one of 'em! Let's see wot 'e can do first—that's all!"

Ben felt that his mother had put the whole problem in a nutshell. He did not really know who Hitler was, and in a confused way wondered—since the sky seemed to be the place to look for trouble—if Hitler might not be a new and more aggressive type of God. God, even the less aggressive and more agreeable kind, had never come much Ben's way before; but he had heard vaguely of Somebody in the Sky who could interfere, but rarely did, with what went on in Beulah Street.

The Lady was evidently very much afraid of this indefinite Person. Her eyes filled with a strained and anxious kindness. She held out her beautifully gloved small hand to his mother and said, "Well, if it gets bad—if they do start bombing London this autumn, I shall come back and ask you again! Meanwhile, do at least send Alfred and Violet! Goodbye, Ben!" . . .

A car drove up for the Lady, one of those great, soft luxury cars that Ben knew he would never see more of than its polished shell. She stepped into it, and was borne away to that secure world belonging to her—but with a heart far more anxious for their safety than were the hearts she had left behind her.

"Well there," said Mrs. Barton with astonished pride, "that *was* a Lady, Ben—an' no mistake! It might 'ave been the Queen 'erself from the clothes on 'er; but bless you—it's wot I always tells yer father—they don't mean no 'arm by it!"

The second interview selected takes place near the end of the book. It is again between Mrs. Barton and the Vision and with Ben present. It is the first time that Mrs. Barton has seen the Vision since the earlier interview.

In the interim bombs have rained day and night, the Barton flat has been destroyed, and Ben and Mabel are in the hospital recovering from having been buried two days in the basement of a bombed building, whence they had been miraculously rescued. The interview takes place in the hospital.

After the first interview the twins had been sent to Cornwall, but Mrs. Barton had been unable to part with Ben.

Ma was invited to go to the housekeeper's room to have a talk with the Vision. Ben was not supposed to be present at this interview; but he wangled it somehow out of Nurse Rosamund.

"Ben is getting on splendidly," the Vision said kindly, "all his cuts are healing up; but we think he ought to have another week's rest before he travels. Mabel needs *quite* that. The younger they are, the more shock affects their bodies rather than their minds.

"What I really wanted to ask you, Mrs. Barton, is what you intend to do now? I feel sure you won't want to have Mabel and Ben back in Dockland again—with the conditions what they are? It was a Mercy of Heaven they were twice saved, but we can't count on further miracles."

"Yus, they do siy as 'ow the third time is fatal," Mrs. Barton agreed with apparent calm, "an' yer carn't count on nuffin', that's true too. Reg'lar as clock-work, those C-rains go orf up our way. I tell you strite, it *is* in my mind that the children orter be somewheres else! I wudn't send them over the seas—where I cudn't git ter them, no matter wot 'appened—but I don't mind sendin' of 'em to Cornwall. The Twins is orl right there seemingly."

"There's one difficulty about sending the children alone," the Vision said reflectively. "Mabel can't go without you. She's too young. You see, in the Government scheme, children must be evacuated *with* their mothers unless they are school age. You see the sense of that don't you? Now, if you'll all three go, I think I could get a cottage where the Twins could join you—near where they are now."

Ben pressed his mother's knee with his hard fist. His eyes worked themselves into her troubled face like gimlets. Surely—surely, she could but agree to this perfect plan—she had only to stop being troubled? Hadn't he a right to her—to his own mother—hadn't Mabel—and the Twins? Didn't people always say, "Children first," if there was a shipwreck; and hadn't they had what amounted to a shipwreck?

117

The Vision, too, was on his side. Ben knew that; he could feel her wanting it. Mrs. Barton's lips worked. She put her hand over Ben's fist, and held it so tight that it hurt.

"It's this way," she said painfully, "your children—well, they need you any'ow, don't they—young or old they need you! An' you've got ter think of 'em all rahnd like. The older ones—my Flossie and Bert—they ain't got no one else ter see after 'em, if I'm not there. Nor they wudn't take anythin' in the way of looking after, from no one else. Not that they'd take it from me always —but you know wot I mean! They do *look* to their mother! But the young ones, my Ben and Mibel, an' the Twins—well, there'd be people ter see after them! Whether or no, they *git* looked after! You yourself, Lady, you'd be all aht ter 'elp children firs', wudn't you? An' there's my ole man too! 'Ow's 'e goin' ter break anyone else into 'is wiys? A man like my 'Erbert—'e 'as 'abits; an' 'e 'as a right ter them, 'asn't 'e? 'E's worked 'ard orl 'is life! 'E ain't ser young any more—turned fifty 'e 'as; an' 'e needs someone ter study 'im. 'E gits them brownkill colds every winter, an' 'oo's ter look after 'im then? Flossie, she 'as ter 'ave fun like any other young girl. You carn't tie them up to their payrints —sick or well—an' I wouldn't want ter! I've thort it orl aht, Ben, ser it ain't no use yer squeezin' my weddin' ring into me flesh—like a Demon! I want ter go erlong of you, with Mibel, jes as much as yer wants ter 'ave me! But fair is fair—yer carn't git away from it. The way I see it is—I *got* ter stiy with Flossie and your Dad, an' keep the 'ome goin'!"

It seemed to Ben that Ma was being both stubborn and wrong. She sat there as red as a beetroot; and there, right in her lap as it were, lay a wonderful new life for all three of them, free from bombs and terrors—and she wouldn't touch it! She wouldn't take her children and go and live in a cottage with nothing to hurt her—and where there was nothing to hurt Mabel. Ben frowned savagely at her. He would have liked to hit her. "If you goes, I go," he told her truculently, "an' if you stiys, Ma, then Mibel an' me stiys wiv yer! Yer carn't stop us!"

The Vision looked pained at this complete repudiation of authority; but she said nothing. She was a sensible woman, and perhaps she realized that the bond between this mother and her son was of so deep a kind that rough words did not shake it. Nor—except in the last resource—would his mother use the weight of authority upon the will of a child so deeply loved and trusted.

"Mrs. Barton, it *is* a very hard choice," she said at last, gently. "May I say just what I think about it, before leaving you to talk it over with Ben? If you decide to take Mabel, I can really get you all together, and all safe—except of course, the three grown-up workers, whom you will have to leave behind. But you do leave them behind together, don't you? Mustn't they learn to be unselfish too? And reasonable? They cannot go—but you can! Would they really like you to risk your life, and the baby's, because they can't stand a few months —or a year or two—of loneliness and inconvenience? Your husband and son should learn to protect your daughter; and she should try to take your place and see after their comfort. That, at least would seem to me the fairest plan, and in the long run—the happiest for you all! Sometimes an outsider like myself can see plainer than the person involved. You feel pulled both ways; and you want

118

to sacrifice your own security—and your baby's—just for their comfort! That hardly seems, to me, right to any of you!"

Mrs. Barton's eyes filled with slow tears, but she said nothing. She just shook hands with the Vision, who was preparing to leave them.

Ben knew that Ma still liked the Lady; she even felt there was sense as well as deep kindness in what she said; but it was no use thinking that his mother was convinced. She was merely shaken; and Ben knew that his mother could be shaken every which way without being convinced.

Still, as their hands met, their hearts met too. Ben saw, with deep approval, that for one strange moment they even looked alike.

Then the Vision was gone and Ben was alone with his mother. She ceased to be moved in quite the same way. She sank back into the armchair, and relaxed. She put her arm round Ben, who leaned against her as if he were a baby, and not a big boy of seven years old.

"You got ter see it the wiy I do, son!" she told him gently. "It's Flossie— it's 'er bein' a young girl like—that's lost her fust young man—an' e' 'er Steady as we orl thort! An' now there's 'er shop bombed aht! Yer farver, 'e means well by orl 'is children. I ain't arsked 'im, but I know 'e'd let me go—if I *did* arsk! 'E's agreed ter sendin' you an' Mabel awiy—but wot'll 'e feel like left alone? Flossie—'oo's she—ter know when ter keep 'im in, in the winter when 'is cough's ser bad, an' when not? Nor 'e wudn't *stiy* 'ome fer Flossie if she *did* know! There's Bert too—'e's going' inter the Navy. Well, that's O.K. by me if 'is 'eart is set on it. But I'd like ter be 'ome fer 'is leaves—even if 'e does spend the most of 'is free time with 'is young lady. Yer see 'ow it is, Ben, these rich folk like this lady—they're good ter their famblies, but it comes easy-like. They can be—an' if they ain't, there's their 'ouses going on sime as usual with meals an' all; or they can piy fer 'otels—or 'ave friends ter stiy wiv. It's wunnerful wot money will do—one wiy or another! I ain't blamin' 'er! You can see she's turned 'er own 'ome into a 'orspital fer orl them pore bombed-aht people as gets 'urt! Well, thet's orl right—'er mind's full of things as mine isn't. I only got my fambly. I sorter fink it's *diff'rent* for 'er! Wot she says *sounds* sense—an' it may be sense for '*er*—but it don't come raw out of 'er 'eart! You can see that, carn't yer, Ben?"

"Well—wot abaht Mibel?" Ben asked with quivering lips and a rebellious spirit. "I don't want Mibel ter git buried againe—an' me not there neither! An' wot yer goin' ter do wiv Mibel while yer at work?"

"I thort of that!" Mrs. Barton told him. "I thort Flossie'd take 'er there mornin's, seein' the shops is later openin' than my offices, and I'd fetch 'er 'ome when I leave my ladies. There's nersery schools they calls 'em, nah—where mothers *can* leave their babies while they goes ter work. Wunnerful good places fer babies they do siy. An' there's one not too far orf—wot I went ter see— cots, an' gimes, an' nice ladies too—lookin' arter them. Mibel'd not 'ave ter be with that minder no more—she got killed any'ow lars' week, in the pub at the corner she wos—sime as usual—*not* mindin' the biby she was pide ter mind! Thet's enuff of minders fer me! But these nersery schools *is* diff'rent, Ben, they is reely!"

"Arrh!" said Ben darkly. "I won't take it! If Mibel stiys, I stiy!"

It broke his mother's heart to repudiate him. "You'd 'ave ter go," she said, "'cos Ben, there ain't no use in yer stiying'! An' wot's more, there's some things I *can* stand—and some I *carn't*. Mibel, I can pick up an' run wiv—she won't get killed if I can 'elp it! Them air raids aren't nuffin' by day. But I jes' carn't stand 'avin' *you* buried one moment an' bombed aht the next! I've 'ad enuff of it!"

There was a long silence. She was the first to break it. She said tentatively, "Well, Ben, 'ave you figgered it orl aht fer yerself—the wiy I said?"

He buried his head against her arm and muttered through hot tears, from the depths of the heart she had built up like her own, on love and courage: "Orl right, Ma, I'll go 'lone—if yer want me to!"

These interviews were chosen because of their timeliness and because they illustrate the difficulties in bridging the gap between the frequently diverse backgrounds of the interviewer and interviewee. Even when these backgrounds are not as fundamentally different socially and culturally as represented here, there is always the problem of establishing "lines of communication" between two individuals unknown to each other.

The author here has given us a vivid account of what went on in Mrs. Barton's mind and of how difficult it was for her to accept the interviewer's evaluations and for her set of values to be understood by the well-meaning Vision. Both were primarily interested in the safety of the children, but they could not see "eye to eye" as to what constituted that safety. To Mrs. Barton, personal care and proximity constituted safety; separation and the unknown were greater threats to her than Hitler's bombs.

The author represents the interviewer as kindly and well-intentioned, but failing because she is unable to understand Mrs. Barton's fear of sending her children away. Her arguments are ineffectual because they do not touch Mrs. Barton's real anxieties. There is no emotional rapport between the two. Mrs. Barton and Ben, by contrast, understand each other's feelings fully and consequently can meet the doubts each has with very little discussion. Because their hearts meet, their minds do also, and Ben "is persuaded."

Especially during the confusing times ahead in this country, every interviewer needs to give particular attention to the human values involved in any plan. Excellent paper plans may be worked out, but unless they take into consideration individual variations and win the emotional acceptance of the client, the necessary participation will be lacking and the plans made useless.

Recapitulation

SOME recapitulation is now in order. In the light of our examination of the concrete interviews above and the illustrations they have furnished of our general discussion of salient characteristics of human psychology, we can review and summarize our suggestions on "how to conduct an interview."

Beginning

No matter how many questions need to be answered, no matter how much information he wishes to impart, the interviewer should always "begin where the client is." After the brief introductory statement as to the manifest purpose of the interview, a few leading questions which will enable the client to express what is on "the top" of his mind will usually be most helpful. Of course the interviewer will have thought over the interview in advance and will know fairly definitely what he wants to obtain from it. But by letting his client talk first, he finds out the client's purpose and is able to pick up many leads as to the best way of getting the information needed to help him. He knows his goals but he will keep his plan of procedure flexible until such "leads" indicate the best course to take.

Somewhere during the interview and often early, the client should be given a fairly clear idea of the sort of things the interviewer and his agency can do to help, and of the sort of responsibility the client himself must assume in meeting his problem. Often the matter can be introduced by asking the client, "In what ways did you think we might be of help?" He needs reassurance that he has come to the right place for help, but he should not be over-assured nor led to feel that he is now relieved of all responsibility, that his problem will be "taken care of." Usually at first a very brief statement of the sort of services the agency tries to render will suffice. Later as the interview proceeds, further explanation of the precise ways in which the agency can help can be given. Often an interviewer finds it useful in closing the interview to run over with the client the next steps each has agreed to undertake.

121

Continuing

After the interviewee has told his story largely in his own way, the interviewer will make use of the clues thus revealed to introduce further questions and discussion in crucial areas so as to fill out the picture and focus the interview on that territory whose exploration promises to be most fruitful. It is at this stage that expert direction of the interview is most called for. The interviewer must decide on the areas to be explored and the best way of drawing out the client concerning them. Indispensable to the successful accomplishment of the latter is the establishment and development of that rapport between the client and himself which will give the client confidence in his unselfish desire to help and in his possession of the understanding and general knowledge required for effective assistance. This confidence established, he can proceed by careful direction of the course of the conversation to the necessary knowledge of the underlying basic factors of the specific problems of this particular client.

It is not easy to achieve the golden mean of leaving the client free to talk spontaneously and at the same time giving the interview continued direction into fruitful channels. Mere listening and encouragement merely leaves the client floundering in the same sea of uncertainty in which he was lost when he applied for help. But over-direction can stifle the interview in its infancy by preventing the salient features of the matter from rising to clear awareness.

Again it is not easy to achieve the ideal balance between relieving a client of the unbearable burden of what seem to him insurmountable difficulties, and of leaving him with essential responsibility for working out his own destiny. In the interviews we have considered, even where the client was most in need of help, the worker, though doing enough to make the difficulties seem conquerable, has in each case carefully left responsibility and initiative with the client. It is a temptation to work out a solution in full detail, especially when working with children or old people, but this temptation must be resolutely resisted. It is better to have a few details wrong and to have the client feel that the plan is one he has been instrumental in developing and is carrying out, with help to be sure, but essentially on his own initiative.

Closing

In bringing an interview to a close, several things should be kept in mind. It is usually a good plan to end with a recapitulation of "next steps." A tying together of the threads of the interview and a restatement of what interviewer and client are each going to attend to before their next conference is valuable. If possible, a definite next appointment should be made. If the interview has involved considerable expression of emotion, the interviewer can usually avoid an emotional let-down by turning his client's attention to objective factors before closing the interview.

One of the most important skills for an interviewer is a knowledge of his own limitations. To know when to refer a client elsewhere, when to terminate an interview, when to explore an emotional situation and when to leave some area unexplored requires skill that comes only with practice. It is a help to remember that an interviewer seldom aims at a complete personality change for his client; his functions are usually much more limited. He mustn't stop too soon nor too late but at "just the right time." And "the right time" varies from case to case. With growing skill in interviewing, it is selected with increased ease and confidence.

The next few years will bring many new clients to interviewers to seek assistance in meeting the new problems to which these times give rise. Sources of new tensions are everywhere, in the draft, in the rising cost of living, in the need for evacuation of certain areas, in the curtailment of customary freedoms, in the imminent danger of death itself. Skilled interviewers are needed as never before. We realize that such skill cannot be acquired simply by reading a book, but a study of the theory of interviewing and thoughtful consideration in the light of it of one's own practice and experiences in interviewing will help a worker to develop his skill and render increasingly valuable service.